There is a lot to be learned about ADHD, but what I love about *Succeeding With Adult ADHD* is the exercises that help you apply what you've learned. This is too often the missing piece with other books. So, buy this book, learn as much as you can, and throw yourself into the exercises—you'll thank yourself for it.

—Ari Tuckman, PsyD, MBA, *author of* Understand Your Brain, Get More Done: The ADHD Executive Functions Workbook; More Attention, Less Deficit: Success Strategies for Adults With ADHD; *and* Integrative Treatment for Adult ADHD. A Practical, Easy-to-Use Guide for Clinicians

Levrini and Prevatt provide a comprehensive course about ADHD self-regulation that reads more like an interesting conversation. Adults with ADHD will recognize themselves and appreciate the authors' lack of judgment. Professionals who work with these adults—such as college disability service providers—will welcome the clear presentation of practical, evidence-based interventions.

—David R. Parker, PhD, *Postsecondary Disability Specialist, CRG Inc., Indianapolis, IN*

Succeeding With Adult ADHD goes well beyond the typical ADHD self-help book by providing detailed strategies for goal setting, self-motivation, and organization and time management as well as for seeking effective treatment support. Levrini and Prevatt have written a book specifically tailored to meet the needs of adults with ADHD. They offer manageable, brief segments and exercises to help readers directly practice and apply key concepts. I highly recommend this book to adults with ADHD as well as clinicians and educators working with this population.

—George J. DuPaul, PhD, *Department of Education and Human Services, Lehigh University, Bethlehem, PA*

Succeeding
With
Adult
ADHD

Succeeding With Adult ADHD

Daily Strategies to Help You Achieve Your Goals and Manage Your Life

Abigail Levrini, PhD, and Frances Prevatt, PhD

American Psychological Association • Washington, DC

Published by
APA LifeTools
American Psychological Association
750 First Street, NE
Washington, DC 20002
www.apa.org

To order
APA Order Department
P.O. Box 92984
Washington, DC 20090-2984
Tel: (800) 374-2721;
Direct: (202) 336-5510
Fax: (202) 336-5502;
TDD/TTY: (202) 336-6123
Online: www.apa.org/pubs/books
E-mail: order@apa.org

In the U.K., Europe, Africa, and the Middle East, copies may be ordered from
American Psychological Association
3 Henrietta Street
Covent Garden, London
WC2E 8LU England

Typeset in Sabon by Circle Graphics, Inc., Columbia, MD

Printer: United Book Press Inc., Baltimore, MD
Cover Designer: Naylor Design, Washington, DC

The opinions and statements published are the responsibility of the authors, and such opinions and statements do not necessarily represent the policies of the American Psychological Association.

Library of Congress Cataloging-in-Publication Data

Levrini, Abigail.
   Succeeding with adult ADHD : daily strategies to help you achieve your goals and manage your life / Abigail Levrini and Frances Prevatt. — 1st ed.
      p. cm.
   Includes bibliographical references and index.
   ISBN-13: 978-1-4338-1125-8
   ISBN-10: 1-4338-1125-1
   1. Attention-deficit disorder in adults—Popular works. I. Prevatt, Frances F., 1955- II. Title.

   RC394.A85L48 2012
   616.8589—dc23
                                2011036958

British Library Cataloguing-in-Publication Data
A CIP record is available from the British Library.

Printed in the United States of America
First Edition

This book is dedicated to my husband, daughter, and other family members, both human and nonhuman. Without them my goals would mean nothing.
—*Abigail Levrini*

I would like to dedicate this book to my husband, six children, and three grandchildren, who have given me a wealth of experience with active, happy, creative people.
—*Frances Prevatt*

CONTENTS

Succeeding
With
Adult
ADHD

INTRODUCTION

This book was written to help you better manage your adult attention-deficit/hyperactivity disorder (ADHD) so that you can stop feeling frustrated by what you are not accomplishing and start making practical steps toward achieving your goals. We know that there are many adults with ADHD who either don't want or cannot afford professional help; however, that shouldn't stop you from being able to utilize many of the same tools and strategies professionals use with their clients. We also know that there are many self-help books to choose from. In this one you won't find lengthy background notes on what ADHD is; instead, we assume you already know the basics of how ADHD is affecting your life. We assume you have tried many suggestions for managing your ADHD and came up short. So here we offer realistic, proven, and unique strategies to use in your daily life so that you may succeed with adult ADHD.

HOW TO READ THIS BOOK

We have tried to make our book user-friendly and practical. Many individuals with ADHD find that they cannot handle the intensity of some self-help books. Because lack of attention and focus is a cornerstone of the disorder, lengthy or jargon-filled books can be too overwhelming to read. To help make this book easy to read, we have included several means of support.

First, we have organized our book into manageable 5- to 15-minute segments. Visual aids have been inserted showing where

to "Start"  and "Stop" reading.

Also, each chapter is broken down into short, distinctive sections that offer many perspectives on using each tool. Specifically, chapters may contain one or more of the following features:

- *Quiz Yourself—Does This Sound Like You?* "Yes" or "No" questions that will allow you to gauge if that chapter is for you
- *What the Experts Say.* A short, nontechnical interpretation of the latest research on ADHD to help you see the scientific rationale for helping yourself
- *Can You Relate to This?* Case examples of adults with ADHD that help you learn from others' experiences

- *Help Yourself!* A list of tips, checklists, or brief fill-in exercises to help you apply what you have read
- *Try It!* More in-depth exercises or ideas to do on your own at home
- *Getting Back on Track.* Detailed explanations for how to overcome ADHD-related difficulties
- *Chapter Summary.* A checklist of ideas to take away from the chapter. After reading each chapter, use the list to note areas you have thoroughly studied and those you may want to revisit.

WHAT'S IN THE BOOK

The book chapters were selected on the basis of our experiences coaching, counseling, and conducting research with adults who have ADHD. We selected 10 topics that we think are most important in helping you to live a healthy and productive life. We have divided the book into three parts.

In Part I, we teach you how to envision goals for yourself and make realistic plans to achieve those goals. We think setting personal goals is one of the most important strategies you will learn. Everyone's lifestyle and needs are different, so our philosophy in this book is that managing ADHD is about creating a plan that works for *you*. You might decide that you want to be more focused at work, learn how to organize your office, be on time for appointments, improve your social skills, or improve your academic functioning. There are different ways of achieving each of the goals you might set, but the key is to make them *your* goals so that you will have the motivation to attain them.

Chapter 1 is on long-term goals and weekly objectives. We teach you how to initiate change by setting effective goals and then breaking them down into small, achievable steps or objectives.

Chapter 2 is on rewards and consequences. We show you how to apply rewards and consequences to increase your motivation to follow through on the goals you have set. We also look at how you can use metacognition to better understand your behavior and what works best for you.

Part II gives you specific strategies for managing parts of your life in which you likely have goals. In Part II, you will find chapters on time management, academic skills, relationships and social skills, organization, and job or employment skills. Here's a brief overview of what you can find in these chapters.

Chapter 3 is on time management. We give you tools to keep you from procrastinating, we help you to prioritize your tasks, and we help you to plan when and how you will accomplish things. This chapter is a must-read for those who have trouble with starting, continuing, and finishing tasks.

Chapter 4 is on social skills. We go over the ways that inattentiveness, impulsivity, and distractibility can get in the way of your social relationships. We help you figure out if you are realistic in your self-perception of your social skills. The how-to part of this chapter gives you suggestions for paying attention in conversations and teaches you how to make a Listening Plan.

Chapter 5 is on organization. This chapter will help you to begin to organize your environment in a way that makes sense to you as an adult with ADHD. We start with motivators to help you *want* to become more organized and follow with step-by-step strategies for taking charge of your life. There are detailed plans for getting ready, actually organizing, and staying organized once your new system is in place. After reading this chapter, you should be able to develop your own personalized organizational plan.

Chapter 6 is on learning and study skills. We give you very specific strategies for studying, memorizing, paying attention, taking notes, reading without your mind wandering, writing a paper, and taking tests. We also talk about test anxiety and ways to manage it.

Chapter 7 is on employment. We guide you through a process of identifying your strengths and weaknesses. Then we provide specific coping skills to help you with organization and time management at work. We make suggestions for dealing with distractibility and lack of focus during the day and give you information about workplace accommodations to which you might be entitled.

Finally, Part III has three chapters that focus on getting additional help. Some adults with ADHD also struggle with anxiety, depression, or just increased stress. In addition, the medication used to treat ADHD can be confusing to understand or can cause frustrating side effects.

In Chapter 8, we give you advice on dealing with conditions such as anxiety, depression, and stress on your own, and on how to figure out when and how to get outside help.

In Chapter 9, we help you to understand the pros and cons of medication and how to make the most of prescription drugs if you choose this option.

In Chapter 10, we cover alternative treatments that you might consider to help with your ADHD, such as healthy lifestyle options, ADHD coaching, or counseling.

At the end of the book, you will find a list of resources if you want more detailed information on any of the topics covered in the chapters.

First Things First: Get an Accurate Diagnosis

If you are reading this book, you most likely have been diagnosed with ADHD or suspect you have ADHD. If you already have a diagnosis, you might consider whether your evaluation followed best-practice guidelines. If you are considering seeking an evaluation, the following will help you determine how to proceed. ADHD can be diagnosed by a psychologist, a medical doctor, or a psychiatrist (who is actually a specific type of medical doctor). However, it is vitally important that the professional you choose actually specializes in diagnosing ADHD. We are not at the point (yet) at which we can simply scan a person's brain and state conclusively that he or she does or does not have ADHD. For now, the best method of diagnosing ADHD involves gathering multiple sources of data.

Your *medical doctor* plays a large role in ruling out medical factors before any additional evaluation is done. Attentional and behavioral problems resembling ADHD can be caused by medical issues such as diabetes, thyroid disorders, or anemia, to name a few, and it is important that a medical professional evaluate the possibility of such a problem before proceeding. If medical factors are ruled out, you will need a specific evaluation for ADHD. Many physicians do not specialize in the wide array of tests needed for the actual evaluation of ADHD. Proper diagnosis of ADHD is a lengthy process requiring several hours and usually involves tests of intellectual and academic functioning. Ask your physician if he or she specializes in ADHD and, if so, how a diagnosis is made. Some physicians have lots of experience with such disorders and are able to take the time to properly diagnose you. However, if your physician is more of a generalist without an ADHD focus, you may want to ask for a referral.

Similarly, although some *psychiatrists* are able to spend time counseling their clients, advances in medication have lessened this emphasis for most. Instead, many contemporary psychiatrists spend the majority of their time and energy focusing on proper medication management. Their level of expertise with psychotropic drugs far surpasses the knowledge of most general practitioners. They are required to receive extra training regarding medication management. Therefore, it is likely that a psychiatrist will be most helpful after a diagnosis has been made in monitoring your medication should you choose to try prescription drugs as a treatment.

Psychologists who specialize in psychoeducational testing are extensively trained in using the latest tools to diagnose a multitude of disorders and are often the professionals best suited to diagnose you. Again, it is important to choose a psychologist who specializes in evaluations of ADHD. The following summarizes the components of a comprehensive evaluation:

1. An in-depth intake session during which the psychologist goes through a complete medical, social, educational, and psychological history with the client.

2. A behavioral checklist/rating scale to be completed by the client and a spouse, a close friend, a coworker, or another person who sees the adult function outside of the home on a regular basis. These checklists cover common symptoms such as fidgeting, inattention, forgetfulness, or restlessness. Newer checklists measure *executive functioning,* which is a variety of processes that can result in specific impairments in areas such as organization, time management, planning, and emotional functioning.

3. If possible, an interview with people in close contact with the individual. Direct behavioral observations are even better but most often are unrealistic.

4. A measurement of how long one can sustain attention and how impulsive one is, and to distinguish between the three ADHD subtypes. Often this will be a type of "continuous performance test" that might be completed on a computer.

5. Tests of intellectual functioning, cognitive processing, and academic achievement to rule out a possible learning disability or related disorder.

The psychologist will consider all these sources of information, attempt to rule out alternative explanations (such as a learning disability or a psychological disorder), and determine whether you qualify for a diagnosis of ADHD. After your evaluations are completed, the diagnosing professional should conduct a follow-up session with you during which he or she goes over the results of your testing. When you are told of your ADHD diagnosis, make sure you know what "type" you are being diagnosed with: primarily inattentive type, primarily hyperactive/impulsive type, or combined type. The diagnosis you receive will be based on the *Diagnostic and Statistical Manual of Mental Disorders* (known as the *DSM*). We often hear clients say they have ADHD "without the H" or "I have ADD—not ADHD." These statements are technically incorrect, but don't blame yourself for the confusion. Because of frequent changes in the *DSM*, names can be baffling. We've already been through *DSM I, II, III, IV,* and are currently on the *DSM–IV–TR* (TR stands for *text revision*).

If you were diagnosed after 1980 and before 1987, ADD is the name you would have been given. If you have been diagnosed or reassessed for the disorder since the mid-90s, you should fall into one of three categories or "subtypes" of ADHD: predominantly inattentive, predominantly hyperactive/impulsive, or the combined type. Slated to be published in 2013, the *DSM–V* may once again mean significant changes to the definitions. Therefore, by the time you read this, your diagnosis may have been altered once again. Some noteworthy changes being considered include doing away with subtypes and creating two separate disorders for ADD and ADHD, changing the age at which you are required to show symptoms from ages 7 to 12 years, and requiring fewer symptoms to be present for a diagnosis of adult ADD. As of now there are no separate criteria for an adult diagnosis, so this would be a positive and significant change for adults with ADHD.

Many of these changes are based on new research being con- ducted with adults with ADHD. Researchers have discovered that up to 70% of children with ADHD have symptoms that persist into adulthood. However, the way the symptoms manifest and how many symptoms you experience may change. For example, you may have been hyperactive as a child only to find that you no longer fit that type as an adult. You no longer have difficulties with staying seated or blurting out answers. As an adult, you are more likely to be struggling with the inattentive and impulsive features of the disorder, such as an inability to focus on your work, pay attention in conversations, or control your emotions. In summary, to do the best job of managing your ADHD, it's important to get an accurate diagnosis, understand what that diagnosis entails, and rely on professionals who specialize in ADHD.

We hope that you will find the strategies in this book both useful and easy to apply. Although effort is involved any time you attempt to integrate new techniques into your schedule, before long you will find that these ideas have become routine, leading to a life that is more organized, streamlined, and really fits *your* unique personality and goals. So go ahead and turn on some background music, find a comfortable spot, and begin to meet your goals—10 minutes at a time.

Part I

GETTING STARTED: ACHIEVING YOUR GOALS AND OBJECTIVES

 Part I of this book focuses on helping you to pinpoint exactly what behaviors you want to change in your life, to create an effective plan in order to change those behaviors, and then to carry out and modify your plan as you learn more about yourself. Specifically, here are the important lessons you will take away from Part I:

- How ADHD affects your ability to set and reach your goals.
- How to set long-term goals.
- How to create weekly objectives.
- How to increase motivation and follow-through.
- How to better understand what works for you.

CHAPTER ONE

STARTING WITH A PLAN

Even if you are on the right track, you will get run over if you just sit there.

—Will Rogers

You've bought the book, you're ready to tackle items on your to-do list, and you're feeling more motivated than you can ever remember. Your impulse is to take off and initiate movement toward your goals while you're feeling hot—but WAIT! Do not "pass go" before thoughtfully reading the following or you might sabotage your efforts. In order to have the best chances at reaching your goals, you must first learn to create what is considered a "good" goal or one that gives you the best chances of success. For adults with ADHD, it is beneficial to have explicitly stated goals, specific methods for accomplishing goals, and specific time frames for meeting those goals. The more concrete you can learn to make your goals, the more likely you are to accomplish them. Also, by learning how to set effective goals and then break them down into small, achievable steps or objectives, you can gain better control over your life, reduce anxiety, and improve productivity. In this chapter, we teach you how to initiate change by creating this sort of solid foundation. To do this, you must start with two simple but invaluable ideas that will propel you toward making your aspirations a reality:

- Step 1: Set long-term goals (LTGs).
- Step 2: Create weekly objectives.

Still think you can achieve your goals without creating a thoughtful plan? Take the following quiz to see if the ideas in this chapter apply to you. The more "yes" answers you give, the more helpful this chapter will be to you.

QUIZ YOURSELF—DOES THIS SOUND LIKE YOU?

1. Do you have abstract ideas of what you would like to accomplish, such as, "I would like to be better organized"?
2. Do you alternate between going full force toward a goal (e.g., crash dieting and losing several pounds in 1 week) and undoing everything you set in motion (e.g., devouring a large pizza in one sitting)?
3. Is your home littered with old to-do lists or notes meant to inspire you but that ended up serving as coasters?
4. Do you get down on yourself because everyone else seems to be reaching their goals except for you?

WHAT THE EXPERTS SAY

Each of the core characteristics of attention-deficit/hyperactivity disorder (ADHD; inattention, hyperactivity, and impulsivity) can negatively impact your ability to set as well as follow through with goals and objectives. For example, problems related to inattention, such as staying focused and on task, make it difficult to pinpoint a particular goal, even if you have a conceptual idea of what you would like to see happen. More obvious, lack of focus inhibits your capacity to follow a goal through to completion. Hyperactivity and impulsivity have the same effect. For someone who sets out to read a book, for example, the need to move about can unravel all efforts in an instant. Impulsivity can lead the same person astray if something more intriguing becomes available. All of these factors can lead you, as an adult with ADHD, to become easily overwhelmed by the idea of setting and meeting goals. Add past failures to the mix and a 10-foot pole may not be nearly long enough to touch the idea of goal setting.

CAN YOU RELATE TO THIS?

Judith came to us for help with her ADHD symptoms as a 33-year-old graduate student in computer science who had been diagnosed during college. She suffered from anxiety as a result of her ADHD symptoms and was a self-proclaimed perfectionist. Judith felt that she did well on school assignments and test taking. Therefore, her primary goals did not initially involve improving her academic performance. On the other hand, she proclaimed that "everything else was a mess." Judith's living space was in disorder. She had difficulty keeping friends because she did not make a consistent effort, and she was unable to sustain a successful romantic relationship. She also had difficulty maintaining a healthy diet and exercising consistently.

At the outset of treatment, Judith's counselor helped her to establish her LTGs. The counselor did not take at face value Judith's insistence that her goals did not involve academics. Instead, as they explored the issue further, Judith revealed that although she received high grades and tested well, she struggled with time management and procrastination, behaviors that were bound to catch up with her at the next level. Still, the counselor also took into account Judith's priorities and gathered information about her desire to eat healthy and exercise, manage her finances, and plan for the future. The counselor asked open-ended questions and encouraged Judith to expand on the explanations of her goals in order to get a "big picture" view. She also focused on Judith's strengths, so that the discussion was not solely about shortcomings, and she produced some ideas about what Judith was good at. These initial discussions helped the counselor understand how to guide Judith so that she could be successful in reaching her goals, and also helped Judith remain positive about herself. The counselor continued to explore Judith's feelings around her ADHD and offer support, then guide Judith as she narrowed in on her LTGs.

GETTING BACK ON TRACK

The following sections will help you begin to create LTGs (Step 1) and then break them down into smaller, weekly objectives (Step 2). At each step, we use Judith as a case example to illustrate how the step should be applied.

STEP 1: SETTING LTGS

What is an LTG? In simple terms, you can think of an LTG as *an outcome that one desires to achieve*. An LTG can vary in terms of the time it may take to be achieved as well as difficulty of achievement. For example, some coaching clients set what they see as more basic goals, such as keeping their home clean for a period of 4 weeks or paying their bills on time for 1 month. Others set forth more lofty goals, such as going back to school for an advanced degree, working on a relationship, or getting a new job. Most people don't have a hard time coming up with ideas about what they would like to achieve in life. The hard part is getting there—or even knowing where to begin.

Edwin Locke of the University of Maryland, College Park, and Gary Latham of the University of Toronto developed their now famous goal-setting theory, derived from more than 400 scientific studies in industrial/organizational psychology, over a 25-year span. They determined that specific and difficult goals were more effective than vague or easy goals. However, they prefaced this finding with the idea that a person must first possess commitment to the goal and have the ability to attain it, two things you may have problems with as an adult with ADHD. World-renowned psychologist Albert Bandura furthered this idea with his research on *self-efficacy*, the belief people have in their capabilities to produce a desired outcome, and how it relates to goal setting and achievement. He found that task-specific confidence is an important factor as well and that without it, other variables may not matter as much. Self-confidence, too, may be a struggle for you as an adult with ADHD. Because you have most likely experienced years of disappointment in terms of reaching your goals and are therefore reading this book, your self-efficacy or self-confidence has most likely taken a bruising when it comes to goal setting.[1]

Goal-directed behavior occurs when individuals are able to hold an LTG in their awareness and use the abstract image of that goal to guide and direct their actions. For adults with ADHD, this knack does not come easily. Without the capacity to hold a goal in mind with consistency and focus, a person with ADHD may find it increasingly difficult to overcome obstacles as they are presented, further hindering the completion of any LTGs.

The first step toward improving the ability to set and reach your goals is to learn how to create an effective goal. As discovered by Locke and Latham, specificity is an important factor, as is setting a goal that will be somewhat of a challenge to obtain. However, as an adult with ADHD who becomes easily overwhelmed, you will need to balance difficulty with what you can realistically do. Keeping these ideas in mind and taking into consideration the challenges faced by adults with ADHD, we have created three "golden rules" for what makes an effective LTG:

- Make your goal Measurable.
- Make your goal Process Based.
- Make your goal Time Sensitive.

 Now let's take a look at each of these criteria in more depth.

[1]Bandura, A. (1997). *Self-efficacy: The exercise of control.* Stanford, CA: W. H. Freeman.

Making an LTG Measurable

First, let's consider the term measurable, which is analogous to Locke and Latham's *specific*. As we mentioned earlier, most people find it fairly easy to come up with ideas about what they would like to achieve or things about their life they would like to change. Responses from adults with ADHD include the following:

- I want to be better organized.
- I want to manage my time better.
- I want to be less distracted.
- I want to be a better spouse/friend/parent.

Although these are all wonderful things to want for yourself, they are not measurable goals. To make these goals measurable, we need to define them in a way that, after a period of time, allows us to produce an evidenced-based "yes" or "no" answer to the question "Did you accomplish your goal?" In other words, how will we know if you are better organized, manage your time better, are less distracted, or have become a better spouse/friend/parent?

Making an LTG Process Based

Next, let's talk about what it means to make a goal *process based*. Just because an LTG is measurable does not automatically make it process based. Here are some similar goals as those listed previously, only now they are measurable but still not process based:

- I want to have my home office organized 2 months from now.

- I want to create a schedule for the next month of activities.
- I want to read a new book.
- I want to buy my spouse/friend/parent a gift.

Again, these ideas are the beginnings of some quality goals, but the lack of the *process* it takes to get there creates a fatal flaw. Many adults with ADHD have mastered the art of procrastination. Therefore, you may be able to put off organizing your home office for 7 weeks only to stay up for 2 days straight getting it in order, put off reading a book for weeks until your spouse threatens to throw out the television, or pick up a thoughtless gift at the grocery store checkout simply to get the goal of buying a present accomplished. On the other hand, you can work very hard and still not reach your LTG if it is based solely on the achievement of one final outcome. You may spend an hour every day trying to get that home office in order but not quite finish in time, you may diligently read 30 minutes each night and still not finish that book, or you may spend a lot of time thoughtfully considering what gift to buy but still not find quite the right thing. Finally, the major error in regard to the goal of creating a schedule is that it does not mention anything about following through or maintaining that schedule. What good is a schedule if you don't stick to it? Making a goal process based ensures that you will consistently monitor and focus behavior in a way that will help you not only to achieve the LTG but also—and more important—to understand your behavior along the way.

Making an LTG Time Sensitive

This rule is a lot more straightforward. Simply put, you must include a deadline by which time the LTG should be accomplished, otherwise it is left out in oblivion to dangle forever and ever. The trick here is to be realistic. For example, don't think that although you haven't read a book in 2 years, you will be able to read nightly for the next month. People commonly make this mistake when it comes to things like exercise and nutrition as well, which are important parts of ADHD symptom reduction (more on that in Chapter 10 on finding the right counselor, coach, or other support you need to reach your goals). If you haven't set foot in the gym for 5 years, don't aim to run a 10-km (6.3 mile) race in 3 weeks. It's not going to happen. Remember, any amount of goal-directed behavior that you engage in is most likely more than you were doing the week before, and that is something to be proud of. A realistic goal may be to get to the gym once a week for 6 months: You may not see this as ideal, but it is better than not going at all.

Time-management tools such as planners and calendars can help you navigate goals over time (more about time management specifics in Chapter 3 on overcoming procrastination and fear to improve time management). If you are tech savvy, mobile applications such as Goal Tracker can help keep you on course with your goal deadlines.

Keeping the Three Golden Rules in Mind

As you read the following four possible ways to express our original goals, remember the three golden rules (making LTGs that are measureable, process based, and time sensitive). Highlight each part of the LTGs that you think illustrates one of the golden rules:

- I want to create and maintain a system of organization for my home office over the next 3 months.

- I want to utilize an agenda to record my schedule on a weekly basis, then follow through with that schedule for the next 8 weeks.
- I want to research and attempt one new skill per week to help increase my ability to focus for the next 5 weeks.
- I want to dedicate 1 hour per evening to bond with my spouse/help my friend/play with my kids for the next 2 months.

Below are the LTGs created by our case example, Judith, using the three golden rules.

Judith's Long-Term Goals	
What would you like to accomplish? Write a long-term goal (LTG) that is measurable, process based, and time sensitive.	**By when would you like to accomplish this LTG? Pick a definitive due date.**
1 Find appropriate computer science position by creating and following through with a job search timeline.	April 15th (10-week timeline)
2 Create an organizational system for my bedroom and maintain that organization.	April 1st (8-week timeline)
3 Generate a study plan for each of my courses and follow through with that plan.	April 30th (12-week timeline)
4 Eat one more serving of vegetables per day.	April 30th (12-week timeline)

HELP YOURSELF!

Next, create three or four LTGs for yourself that possess the three golden rules (measurable, process based, time sensitive). Prioritize them and write each goal in a separate box. Then write the corresponding "due date" in the right-hand box, next to your LTG.

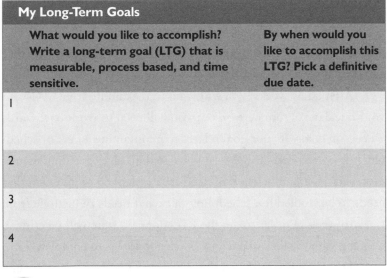

My Long-Term Goals	
What would you like to accomplish? Write a long-term goal (LTG) that is measurable, process based, and time sensitive.	By when would you like to accomplish this LTG? Pick a definitive due date.
1	
2	
3	
4	

 STEP 2: CREATING WEEKLY OBJECTIVES

Once you have created your LTGs, you can begin the task of breaking down your goals into smaller, weekly "baby steps." Because an LTG can seem big and overwhelming, now that it has been recorded, put it aside. Focus on the very first step you will need to take in order to eventually reach your goal. Think small. Think easy. For the first few weeks, your job is to set (and complete) objectives that are well within your capabilities. By doing this, you will increase your confidence, enabling you to slowly take on more and more challenging objectives. For example, if you created a time-management goal centered on using an agenda or planner, your first week's objective may be to go to the office supply store and purchase a planner. If you created a goal to exercise more frequently, maybe your first week's objective is to talk to two active friends about athletic activities that they find fun and interesting.

After a few weeks, you will want to reexamine your LTGs and your due dates. From here on out you will need to work backwards on certain goals. If your goal relates to maintaining a task or schedule, just keep going. However, if your goal involves a definitive final task, such as a family trip that needs to be planned or an exam that needs to be studied for, scheduling out what needs to be done from week to week in order to get the LTG done on time will be critical. Keeping with the idea of exercise, say your goal is to complete a run of 10 km (6.3 miles) in 4 months. The first few weeks you may only run a mile or so just to get the ball rolling with an objective you can easily meet and feel good about. After those first few outings, you will need to map out exactly how many miles per week you need to be running in order to be at your goal in 4 months.

When writing down your weekly objectives, be as specific and detailed as possible. It is not enough to say "run 2 miles." Instead, attempt to specify how, when, where, and what you are going to do: "After work, take 20 minutes to change and stretch. At 6:30, go for

2-mile run from home to the high school and back at an easy pace."
Also, do not feel you need to work on every LTG every week. Tackle
your top priority goals first. You may also have more than one
objective pertaining to only one LTG.

Finally, the art of creating weekly objectives that are "not too
big and not too small" can be a challenge for anyone. Don't hesitate
to enlist the help of a coach, counselor, or friend to help you map
out the process for meeting your goal. Following are the objectives
for the first 2 weeks created by our case example, Judith:

Judith's Week #1 Objectives		
What would you like to accomplish this week toward reaching your long-term goal (LTG)? Write a weekly objective.	Corresponding LTG #	By when would you like to accomplish your objective? Pick a definitive due date.
Decide on a planner or calendar system to use for LTG planning and purchase.	1–3	Friday
Spend 1 hour per evening researching computer science positions and decide on 5 places to apply.	1	Sunday
Take photos of my bedroom and bring to next session to review and explore organizing options.	2	Wednesday
Create a list of vegetables I enjoy to purchase next shopping trip.	4	Wednesday

Judith's Week #2 Objectives		
What would you like to accomplish this week toward reaching your long-term goal (LTG)? Write a weekly objective.	Corresponding LTG #	By when would you like to accomplish your objective? Pick a definitive due date.
Find resume and spend 1 hour for 2 days updating and editing.	1	Wednesday and Thursday
Prepare broccoli dish and create 5 individual servings to freeze. Eat 2 servings this week.	4	Sunday
Follow through with study schedule in new planner. Study no more than 45 minutes before taking a break.	3	Sunday
Purchase 4 small shelves and 4 large bins from container store to prepare for room organization.	2	Friday

HELP YOURSELF!

On the following pages, begin to create your first 2 weeks of objectives as they pertain to at least one of your LTGs. Don't forget to pick a definite due date somewhere within the week to accomplish each objective. Remember: Think small, work backward, and be specific!

My Week #1 Objectives

What would you like to accomplish this week toward reaching your long-term goal (LTG)? Write a weekly objective.	Corresponding LTG #	By when would you like to accomplish your objective? Pick a definitive due date.

My Week #2 Objectives

What would you like to accomplish this week toward reaching your long-term goal (LTG)? Write a weekly objective.	Corresponding LTG #	By when would you like to accomplish your objective? Pick a definitive due date.

TRY IT: "STRUCTURED PROCRASTINATION"!

One of our clients taught us a goal-writing technique that she called *structured procrastination.* She described it like this:

> I found it helpful having an objective I can distract myself from another objective with. It gives me structure in how to procrastinate. Like, if I know I have an objective to read but don't want to at that moment, I look and see if there is another objective I'd rather work toward. Last weekend I cleaned my car in order to procrastinate on my reading assignment. If I didn't have that objective, I'd likely have found something else to procrastinate with and I would still be at the same point study wise. So this way I can still procrastinate but it's productive. It works terrific!

By being skillful about the way time-sensitive objectives are written, you can in essence set up activities to do that will allow you to put off other less desirable activities, yet you can always feel you are accomplishing something. In line with the coaching philosophy, you can use this technique to fit your program to your strengths and innate tendencies. Rather than completely fight the urge to procrastinate, you can frame it as a coping strategy.

SUMMARY

Here are the important points you will want to take away from this chapter. Use the following checklist to note the areas you have thoroughly studied. Leave the box empty if it is an area that you would like to come back to and review further.

☐ I understand how ADHD impacts my ability to set and reach goals.

☐ I have learned how to set and use LTGs.

☐ I understand and can apply the three golden rules for an effective LTG.

☐ I have learned how to create and use weekly objectives.

☐ I have applied the idea of structured procrastination for my objectives.

CHAPTER TWO

USING INCENTIVES AND UNDERSTANDING YOUR BEHAVIOR

Nothing is worth doing unless the consequences may be serious.
—George Bernard Shaw

 Now that you have created your long-term goals and weekly objectives, you may be thinking, "Okay, NOW I get started, right?" Well, no. If only it were that simple—design a well-laid plan and follow through. Voila! Goals achieved! Let's not forget that lack of motivation, especially over time, is a fundamental issue for adults with ADHD. Therefore, you'll probably need some help finding enough drive to follow through with the terrific goals you have produced. To help increase and maintain motivation, adding external rewards and consequences for achieving your goals is an integral next step. Last and perhaps most important is an idea called *metacognition*—as you work toward your goals from week to week, you must be thinking through the process and evaluating what works and what doesn't. This practice ultimately assists you in knowing when to apply what skill for not only current but also future goals. This chapter contains the final two steps necessary to successfully achieve your goals as an adult with ADHD:

- Step 3: Add Rewards and Consequences to increase motivation.
- Step 4: Use Metacognition to discover what works.

QUIZ YOURSELF—DOES THIS SOUND LIKE YOU?

Take the following quiz to see if this chapter will be helpful to you. Remember, more "yes" answers means this chapter will be more helpful!

1. Do you feel like you know what you need to do, but you can't get yourself to actually do it?
2. Do you struggle to do things you find boring, uninteresting, or tedious?
3. Are you waiting for that sense of drive to kick in that other people seem to have?
4. Does it feel like you are just going through the motions, repeating the same (unhelpful) behavior patterns over and over?

WHAT THE EXPERTS SAY

In his book, *ADHD and the Nature of Self-Control*, internationally recognized ADHD authority Dr. Russell Barkley argued that the fundamental deficit in individuals with ADHD is one of self-control and that problems with attention are a secondary characteristic of the disorder. For most individuals, as they develop, control of behavior gradually shifts from external sources to a set of internal rules and standards. Young children, not yet

> **Self-Regulation:** The process of consciously managing one's behavior by planning, monitoring, or evaluating, and without the need for external control.

possessing this internal sense of self-control, often act on impulse unless presented with an external reinforcer in the form of a punishment or reward. For example, let's say Timmy, who is 3 years old and does not have ADHD, hits his baby brother, Toby, when he catches Toby using his favorite toy truck. Timmy's mom then tells Timmy that if he hits Toby again he will have a "time out." On the other hand, if he plays nicely with Toby for the next 20 minutes, they will all have ice cream. Timmy is then able to suppress his impulse to hit Toby. His sense of self-control is governed by the external factors his mom presented—time out and ice cream.

Now imagine that Timmy is 14, and Toby has taken his laptop computer without permission. Timmy's initial thought may be to give his brother a good smack, but he refrains. This time his mom isn't around, and no external factors have been presented to him. Instead, Timmy's inner monologue goes something like this:

> If I hit Timmy I will hurt him. I love my brother and I don't want him to hurt. Also, mom and dad would be upset with me, and I don't want to disappoint my parents. I won't solve anything by hitting Timmy—I'll talk to him instead.

35

Here, Timmy has learned to inhibit his behavior on the basis of a set of internal controls and guidelines.

Dr. Barkley argued that the critical deficit associated with ADHD is the failure to develop this capacity for self-control, otherwise known as *self-regulation*. As a result, people with ADHD struggle with goal-directed behavior even as adults. You may have a vague idea of what needs to be done but lack the ability to create and follow through with a specific, well thought out plan and instead get sidetracked and pulled in different directions. Dr. Barkley would argue that to remedy this struggle, treatment should focus on helping you to apply the knowledge you already have at the appropriate times, rather than on teaching specific knowledge and skills. We would argue that it takes both. Just as even a young Timmy was able to regulate his behavior by drawing on external reinforcers, adults with ADHD, such as you, who may not already possess certain coping skills, can also learn to achieve their goals and gain an internal sense of self-regulation.

GETTING BACK ON TRACK

Despite this issue with self-regulation, adults with ADHD can learn to self-motivate—it just may take a little something "extra" at times: the proverbial carrot and stick, so to speak. In this section you will learn how using rewards and consequences (Step 3) is essential to the goal-reaching process and, finally, how metacognition (Step 4) can help you better control future behavior.

STEP 3: ADD REWARDS AND CONSEQUENCES TO INCREASE MOTIVATION

Motivation is characterized as the willingness or desire to be engaged and commit effort to completing a task and is a fundamental struggle for adults with ADHD. Behaviorally, motivation

> **Motivation:** The willingness or desire to be engaged and commit effort to completing a task.

is indicated by a person's choice to engage in a particular activity and the intensity of his or her effort and persistence for that activity.

As much as you hope and wish that "feeling good" about accomplishing something will be enough to motivate you toward a goal, the simple fact is that people with ADHD often need something outside of themselves to dangle—at least in the beginning. There may be individuals walking this earth who get an internal sense of gratification from a clean load of laundry, but we have never come across one of those people with an ADHD diagnosis.

Thinking back to Barkley's self-regulation theory, we know that individuals with ADHD have trouble controlling their behavior. Similarly, individuals with ADHD are attuned to immediate rewards and consequences and often pursue attractive short-term alternatives to their desired goal. For example, you may set an objective for yourself to pay your bills after dinner but see that your favorite movie is playing on TV. Minutes later you find yourself in your pajamas with a bowl of popcorn in front of the television. As you should know by now, this is not a "willpower" problem but a core component of the disorder. Therefore, to help yourself to achieve a desired goal or objective, you need to enhance the motivation. To meet the behavioral expectations that have been set, you must provide rewards and consequences for meeting those expectations that are more attractive and appealing than those associated with alternative behaviors. In other words, tell yourself that if you pay your bills, you will reward yourself with something even better than your favorite *old* movie, such as seeing that blockbuster new movie at the theater later that night. And if not, you will require something of yourself that you would rather avoid at all costs, such as vacuuming one room per bill that goes unpaid.

Many ADHD counselors and coaches regularly use a system of rewards and consequences with clients to help them attend sessions and successfully achieve weekly objectives—and likewise their long-term goals. When studying the impact of ADHD coaching, research has shown that many individuals find learning how to accept and use goals with rewards and consequences the most helpful part of the coaching process. Interestingly, these same individuals often express the most doubt about the system before coaching begins. In his final session, a client named Keith stated that the rewards and consequences were "working pretty well, surprisingly!" and that he remembered that "the first thing I said about that was like, okay . . . I *guess.*"[1]

---

[1]Reaser, A. (2008). *ADHD coaching and college students*. Available at http://etd.lib. fsu.edu/theses/available/etd-04102008-112843/

FACTORS TO CONSIDER WHEN CREATING A SYSTEM OF REWARDS AND CONSEQUENCES

Be complementary. The most effective rewards and consequences are those with relevance to a particular objective or goal. In the coaching study mentioned above, Amanda paired an exercise goal with a consequence of "no ice cream," an end result that would further promote healthy living. Sam paired a budgeting goal with a consequence of "giving $20 to charity," both of which involved spending money responsibly.

The sooner the better. The immediacy with which rewards or consequences are delivered will affect how well they work. For example, if you complete your housework on Monday, don't tell yourself that you will go to the movies 4 or 5 days later on the weekend as a reward. This type of delay would require the sense of internal self-regulation that people with ADHD simply aren't built with. Instead, immediately after completing your housework, pop in a DVD and watch it that night.

Get creative. As you begin to think of ideas for rewards and consequences, take a week and see what you are doing or gravitating toward instead of what you should be doing or are avoiding. The more obvious ideas that come out of this include watching TV, using the computer, using a cell phone, listening to music, or visiting with a friend. These can be great and useful ideas, but if you dig a little deeper you can come up with some far more creative and therefore more fun ideas to work with. For example, a coaching client named Patty always found herself getting angry and embarrassed by a neighbor who had a collection of tacky lawn ornaments in her yard.

Then one day it hit her: "If I don't complete this objective, I will put a tacky lawn ornament in my yard for a week!" The neighbor, with whom she had become friendly, then politely agreed to remove one of her ornaments as a reward for Patty. It worked great! Another client, Ainsley, was always dressed beautifully and wore a perfect coat of make-up to every session. Her counselor suggested that if she completed her objectives, she treat herself to a spa treatment but if not, she go to work without make-up and wearing mismatched clothes. She never missed a single objective.

Try both and then use what works. Despite evidence that external incentives are helpful to adults with ADHD, you may find that either the rewards or consequences aren't motivating. This can happen for a variety of reasons. For example, a client named Jim stated that, "No matter what, I had to complete these goals" and therefore, the rewards held no weight. And Sharon felt that she had "found it difficult to come up with something I could reward myself with because I do that already." Furthermore, clients with anxiety or depression sometimes find the extra pressure of fulfilling a consequence or even a reward can make symptoms and behavior worse. Therefore, you should begin by using both rewards and consequences but then decide whether both are motivating, one works better than the other, or both cause added stress, and adjust accordingly. However, before jumping to conclusions, remember to consider whether the weight of the rewards and/or consequences were heavy or salient enough. You may just need to change the reward or consequence itself, not drop it altogether.

This isn't a bribe. Although it may feel that way, the point of rewards and consequences is not to bribe you or reward you for doing something you should be doing to begin with. ADHD is not an excuse for personal accountability. Instead, the idea is that by putting emphasis on particular objectives and creating a structure with immediate feedback, you can begin to internalize a sense of self-regulation not previously experienced.

TRY IT! CREATE A LIST OF IDEAS FOR REWARDS AND CONSEQUENCES

Remember that *rewards* can be things you currently do or have that you enjoy (computer, make-up, reading), things you would like to do or have (new clothes, see a movie), or things that you don't enjoy that you would like to have taken away (chores). Below, list some possible rewards.

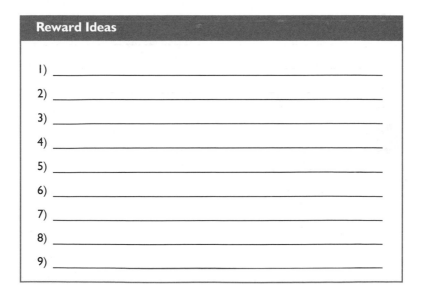

Reward Ideas
1) _____
2) _____
3) _____
4) _____
5) _____
6) _____
7) _____
8) _____
9) _____

Remember that *consequences* can be things that you currently do or have that you don't enjoy but may benefit you (chores, eating healthfully, exercise, saving money), things that you would not like to do or have but may benefit you (same as above), or things that you enjoy that you wouldn't like to have taken away (TV, phone, make-up, money, snacks).

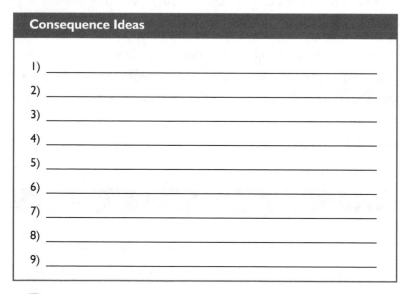

Consequence Ideas

1) _____

2) _____

3) _____

4) _____

5) _____

6) _____

7) _____

8) _____

9) _____

Below are the rewards and consequences used in our case example from Chapter 1, Judith, in her Week 1 objectives:

Judith's Week # 1 Objectives			
What would you like to accomplish this week toward reaching your long-term goal (LTG)? Write a weekly objective.	LTG #	Due date	Reward and/or consequence
Decide on a planner or calendar system to use for LTG planning and purchase.	1–3	Friday	Reward: Decorate planner with favorite photos. Consequence: Decorate planner with embarrassing photos of myself.
Spend 1 hour per evening researching computer science positions and decide on 5 places to apply.	1	Sunday	Reward: Favorite TV show on Sunday evening with a glass of wine. Consequence: No make-up to work on Monday morning.
Take photos of my bedroom and bring to next session to review and explore organizing options.	2	Wednesday	Reward: Buy a new pair of earrings to organize. Consequence: Clean bathroom well including floor and shower.
Create a list of vegetables I enjoy to purchase next shopping trip.	4	Wednesday	Reward: Add diet coke to shopping list. Consequence: Eliminate cookies from shopping list.

HELP YOURSELF!

Using the Weeks 1 and 2 objectives from before, add a reward and/ or consequence for each objective you listed. Use the worksheets below:

My Week #1 Objectives			
What would you like to accomplish this week toward reaching your long-term goal (LTG)? Write a weekly objective.	LTG #	Due date	Reward and/or consequence

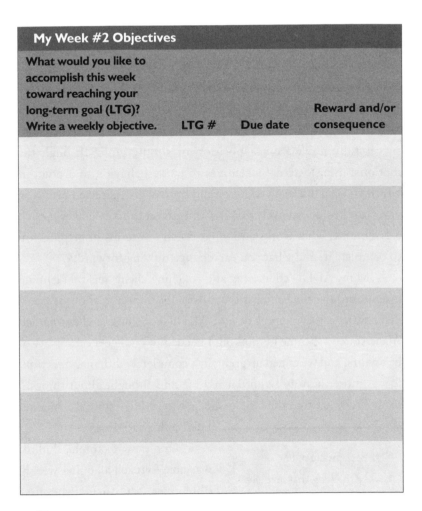

My Week #2 Objectives

What would you like to accomplish this week toward reaching your long-term goal (LTG)? Write a weekly objective.	LTG #	Due date	Reward and/or consequence

STEP 4: USE METACOGNITION TO DISCOVER WHAT WORKS

Metacognition refers to higher order thinking that involves active regulation over the cognitive processes engaged in learning. Literally, metacognition means "thinking about thinking." In order to successfully move from a position of simply going through the motions, using external incentives to guide behavior, to a point at which you can internally monitor and control goal-directed behavior, you must begin to actively think. Think about the way you approach a given task, what works and what doesn't in terms of helping you to complete it, and what you can change moving forward.

Many ADHD counseling and coaching clients feel that gaining insight into their behavior is the most important aspect of the treatment process.[2] On completion of ADHD coaching, a client named Alicia stated, "I came in thinking I needed to change a certain set of behaviors, and we ended up going in a completely different direction. It was more the way I approached life and thought about things." Henry, too, felt that the insights he learned were "kind of a missing link" in his progress.

> **Metacognition:** Higher order thinking that involves active regulation over the cognitive processes involved in learning.

Our case example, Judith, was able to reach all of her weekly objectives set during the first 2 weeks of treatment. By being asked how this made her feel, Judith felt encouraged to take plea-

---

[2]Reaser, A. (2008). *ADHD coaching and college students*. Available at http://etd.lib.fsu.edu/theses/available/etd-04102008-112843/

sure in her success and tie her behaviors to her feelings and cognitions. Because of her small initial successes, Judith began to feel encouraged about moving forward. By having Judith set small objectives in the beginning, her counselor helped her to increase the likelihood that she would be successful in reaching those objectives, and as a result, Judith gained confidence in the process and her abilities. Still, she expressed some concern for her capacity to "keep the momentum going," so her counselor kept this in mind and helped her to continue to experience success.

Every few weeks, Judith and her counselor looked back at her long-term goals that they had set and discussed where Judith felt she had and had not made progress and whether she was on track with her weekly objectives as far as reaching her goals. When examining your own goals and objectives, you may realize that you have been unrealistic with your expectations and need to tone them down. Or you may feel you could do more. Fortunately for Judith, she found her goals to be realistic and achievable. For those who are not as positive, it is important to continuously reevaluate the small steps that should be taken toward realizing a bigger goal and celebrate small achievements. In treatment sessions, modeling a problem-solving strategy is imperative. ADHD counselors and coaches must consistently review previous plans, determine which are workable, and help clients like Judith to adjust goals or behaviors as needed.

Eventually Judith, who had been very successful for the first several weeks, was unable to follow through with one of her objectives. Her counselor acknowledged this but did not at first focus too much on it. Instead, she let Judith continue talking through her other objectives and congratulated her on her successes. It was important that Judith celebrate the positive strides that she had made and not become discouraged with minor setbacks. Only after discussing the other objectives did her counselor bring up the uncompleted objective. A failed objective can be a very valuable learning experience. By facing her fear and admitting that she was unsuccessful, Judith saw that the "world won't end" and that she could continue to persevere in the face of failure. Often adults with ADHD begin to unravel when they hit a roadblock or their motivation starts to fade. Understanding that you don't have to start from square one and that one failure does not undo all of your success can be one of the most valuable lessons learned when working toward your goals.

Steps 1 through 3 (making your goal measurable, making your goal process based, adding rewards and consequences to increase motivation) must be attempted in order to begin engaging in metacognitive strategies. Using the Week 1 worksheet you created previously, attempt to follow through with your first week's objectives, then think back on your week. You may want to use a counselor, coach, or buddy to fully examine your behavior. Then, follow the outline below:

1. First, review the previous week's goals and whether they were met.
2. If goals were not met, think about why you were unable to meet them and whether consequences were enforced.
3. If goals were not met and consequences were not enforced, think about why this occurred and what needs to be changed so that it will not happen again.
4. If goals were met, think about why you were able to do this and whether rewards were carried out.

5. If goals were met and rewards were carried out, think about why this occurred and what needs to happen so that you can continue to be successful.

6. If goals were met but rewards were not carried out, think about why this occurred and what needs to be changed so that you can carry through on rewards.

7. After thinking about the previous weeks' goals, decide on the following week's goals, as well as the rewards and consequences for meeting or not meeting each goal.

TRY IT! DAILY LOG OF GOAL-RELATED ACTIVITIES

The Daily Log of Goal-Related Activities can help you gain further insight into your behavior. To use it, choose one or two objectives during the week and then document your behavior in relation to those objectives.

At the end of their time working together, Judith shared with her counselor some of her final thoughts about the goal-setting process and how she would use her new skills moving forward:

> I got a lot just from the process of writing things down and thinking about my behaviors. What I plan to do at this point is write my objectives on my calendar. For example, "pay bill by this day" or "complete my paper by this day." I will pick a day and a time and a specific moment when it has to be done. Not just like, "oh, this week sometime" or "soon." That way I can't put it off. Something else I think I'll take from it is the steps. Specifically, here is how I start. Here is the next thing I do. And I like to check things off and make lists so that is kind of fun, almost. I feel like I'm getting somewhere. So putting things in small little chunks will probably work for me, going forward. And I'll continue to do that.

Daily Log of Goal-Related Activities				
Specific actions/ behaviors I planned to follow through with today.	Specific steps I took toward following through with set plans.	What helped me follow through with set plans?	Specific steps I did NOT take toward following through.	What obstacles prevented me from following through?

In regard to rewards and consequences, Judith learned this about herself:

> Maybe something I should work on is not rewarding myself so freely. I found that consequences were better motivators for me. I can't reward myself with money because it's my money. I don't want food because that's one of my issues. I tend to do that anyway. So what could affect me negatively was more of a motivator than what I could gain.

Several weeks later, Judith emailed her counselor the following note:

Hi!

I hope you are doing well!

Some updates I thought I'd share: I graduated on Friday with my computer science degree and received an academic award. I was in the top three in my class, can you believe it?! I also received an excellent job offer, which was a direct result of one of the online applications I sent for our weekly objectives. Today is my fourth session with a personal trainer to get me to the gym—I did this because of the success I found having specific days and times for weekly objectives. A trainer keeps me on schedule with days, times, and appointments and I also have to answer to someone. So far it's been working great and it is definitely a result of things I learned in treatment. Just thought I'd share, and say Thank You!!

—Judith

SUMMARY

Here are the important points you will want to take away from this chapter. Use the following checklist to note the areas you have thoroughly studied. Leave the box empty if it is an area you would like to come back to and review further.

☐ I understand the impact of poor self-regulation on my behavior.

☐ I know how to apply rewards and consequences to increase my motivation.

☐ I have used metacognition to better understand my behavior.

☐ I have asked myself specific questions about my plan in regard to what works and what doesn't work for me.

☐ I have used the Daily Log of Goal-Related Activities to get a clearer picture and further insight into my behavior.

Part II

SPECIFIC STRATEGIES

 Part II of this book focuses on typical areas of struggle for adults with ADHD—those areas in which you may want to develop specific goals. Whether you are attempting to obtain a college or advanced degree, navigate the world of work, keep your home life in order, or improve your relationships, this section provides guidelines for getting there. Specifically, here are the important lessons you will take away from Part II:

- How to improve your academic and learning skills.
- How to change your social behavior and make relationships more satisfying.
- How to organize your space and keep it that way.
- How to manage your time more effectively.
- How to find the right career or improve your current job proficiency.

CHAPTER THREE

OVERCOMING PROCRASTINATION AND FEAR TO IMPROVE TIME MANAGEMENT

I love deadlines. I like the wooshing sound they make as they fly by.
        —Douglas Adams, *Hitchhikers Guide to the Galaxy*

One of the biggest concerns held by many adults with ADHD is the inability to manage time well. Some individuals complain of trying to jam too much into the day and never getting to the end of their to-do list. Others can't remember what they are supposed to be doing and end up missing out on important events. Still others know what they should be doing but choose to engage in low-priority activities that are more fun. Poor time management is a form of disorganization. In Chapter 5, we focus on organization in terms of physical "stuff or things," but here in this chapter we focus on organizing the slightly more abstract, cerebral idea of time.

Effective time management is not as easy as it sounds. In this fast-paced, overscheduled society that we live in, even adults without ADHD often struggle to get everything done. Furthermore, time management is not a skill traditionally taught in our homes or schools, leaving most of us to our own devices to navigate our hectic lives. However, when this rudimentary skill is mastered, it can provide a sense of freedom and confidence that can positively affect many other areas of life.

In this chapter, we help you to use techniques to manage your time more effectively. To assist you in accomplishing this task, we have included case examples of clients who have struggled with time management, ways to help you gain insight into your procrastination style or "type," a discussion on how fear is related to poor time management, specific tools and strategies to use in your daily life, detailed instructions on using some of these tools, and fill-in exercises to help you create and implement your own plan.

QUIZ YOURSELF—DOES THIS SOUND LIKE YOU?

1. Do you procrastinate on everything, putting off tasks until an unwanted consequence has you scrambling to get it done, leaving you stressed and regretful?
2. Are loved ones often upset with you because you commit to doing something and then find you are "too busy" to follow through?
3. Do you have trouble prioritizing the things you need to do?
4. Do you create daily to-do lists with several items and only manage to cross one or two off at the end of the day?

5. Do you over- or underestimate how long a task will take and attempt to do too much at one time?

6. Does your boss or colleague have to hassle you to get work turned in on time?

7. Do you find yourself putting off items that should be taken care of immediately, such as paying bills to do something unimportant like rearranging your sock drawer?

8. Do you have trouble starting, continuing, or finishing tasks?

9. Does it feel like everyone around you is getting done three times as much as you in the same amount of time?

WHAT THE EXPERTS SAY

Generally, the more structure and routine incorporated into the life of an adult with ADHD, the better. In addition, setting specific time frames for meeting goals will help you to achieve those goals more quickly and easily. Implementing time management strategies targeting both big and small tasks can help you, as an adult with ADHD, gain better control over your life, reduce anxiety, and improve productivity.

Research on adults with ADHD has shown that individuals who are most successful at reaching their goals are those who are able to follow the regime of breaking down their objectives into small steps and setting strict timelines for completing their objectives. One study participant named Evelyn felt that the "process of making little steps and listing what it would take to meet the larger agenda made things much more manageable." Along related lines, those individuals who consistently write in and follow planners or calendars meet more objectives than those who cannot manage to keep some type of planning device.[1]

Popular and effective choices for time management include monthly desk calendars with large boxes to write in or notebook-sized planners with 15-minute increments printed for each day. Monthly calendars have a valuable "in your face" characteristic. On the other hand, 15-minute planners create a visual representation of time and help with micromanaging. Still other individuals fare better with more "high-tech" time management options. All of these helpful devices are discussed in more detail later on in this chapter.

Another important research finding is that individuals who find "micromanaging" their goals and keeping a planner too rigid and overwhelming are less successful in obtaining their objectives. For example, Susan, who had a history of getting easily overwhelmed by details, felt that it "freaked her out a little bit." If you or your loved one is unable or unwilling to break down goals or objectives into more precise and manageable steps, or to consistently record assignments on some type of calendar, this may indicate that you will have a more difficult time getting everything accomplished. It may also mean that you are struggling with a high degree of anxiety in addition to your ADHD symptoms, which should be addressed. A professional coach or therapist can help teach you the skill of scheduling and how to apply the methods set in this chapter if you have difficulty doing so on your own. If you feel you may be suffering from anxiety, read Chapter 8 on understanding and treating conditions that can coexist with ADHD.

---

[1]Reaser, A. (2008). *ADHD coaching and college students.* Available at http://etd.lib. fsu.edu/theses/available/etd-04102008-112843/

WHY DO I PROCRASTINATE? IDENTIFY YOUR "TYPE"

Procrastination can be defined as the tendency to put off that which is necessary to reach your goals. In 2006, Joseph Ferrari of DePaul University and Sarah Sanders of Illinois School of Professional Development published one of the first studies specifically aimed at exploring the relation between measures of procrastination and adult ADHD.[2] They compared three measures of procrastination between two groups: a sample of men and women with diagnosed ADHD and a sample of men and women attending a public presentation on procrastination. The adults diagnosed with ADHD reported significantly more procrastination as related to decision making and behavior.

To tackle the issue of procrastination head on, it is important to first understand why you procrastinate. The following scenarios describe five reasons why you may be putting things off. You may see yourself in one, some, or all of these scenarios. Read them carefully, then use the space provided to write down your procrastination style(s), personal examples of each, and a brief description of one thing you can do to try to procrastinate less.

Homer Simpson—The Ineffective Prioritizer

Ineffective-prioritizer type procrastinators attend to those tasks that are most convenient, salient, or interesting. In essence, prior-

---

[2]Ferrari, J. R., & Sanders, S. E. (2006). Procrastination rates among adults with and without AD/HD: A pilot study. *Counseling and Clinical Psychology, 3,* 2–9.

59

Procrastination styles:

- Ineffective-prioritizer
- Forgetful
- Easily distracted
- Big picture
- Perfectionist

ity is sacrificed for ease. The problem is that although these easy tasks are being attended to, other tasks begin to pile up, and soon an excess of important responsibilities has been overlooked. Eventually, all of the tasks become urgent—both the backlog of old tasks and imminent new ones—causing stress and confusion. The ineffective-prioritizer type procrastinator is then forced to drop current tasks to attend to the urgent ones, barely squeaking by. When this happens, your priority becomes what is urgent; however, the tendency to want to engage in those nonurgent, nonpriority tasks still exists. An endless cycle ensues: The ineffective-prioritizer type procrastinator becomes bound to pressing issues, is therefore unable to establish the appropriate priorities, and constantly seeks to reduce stress by attending to tasks that are neither urgent nor priority.

Homer Simpson's character on *The Simpsons* consistently deals with this challenge. He'll often promise his wife, Marge, that he will complete an important task for her and then finds himself sitting at the bar in Moe's Tavern instead. At the end of the episode, he is often feeling remorseful and trying to make amends for his poor decisions. Needless to say, taking the time to create and stick to a well-laid plan and completing the most pressing tasks first will help resolve the problems of an ineffective prioritizer.

Silly Ol' Bear—The Forgetful Type

Many individuals with ADHD also struggle with poor working memory. Working memory is a system for temporarily storing and managing the information required to perform complex cognitive tasks such as learning, reasoning, and comprehension. No matter how well these individuals plan and prioritize, problems with memory often keep them from accomplishing their goals. Winnie the Pooh, that loveable childhood classic, frequently struggles with working memory issues. In one of his adventures, "Pooh Goes Visiting and Pooh and Piglet Nearly Catch a Woozle," Pooh sets out a honey jar to try and catch a Woozle, then, forgetting what he has done, finds himself caught in the jar while attempting to get to the honey for himself. Of course, this leads Piglet to think there is a nonexistent Woozle inside and Christopher Robin to once again declare, "Silly Ol' Bear!" Because Pooh was unable to store the fact that he had put out the honey for the Woozle, he was unable to reason that he should not attempt to eat it himself.

Several tricks can help you remember things better. Post-It notes or messages on the bathroom mirror, writing things on your hand, or setting alarms on a cell phone can all be helpful. However, the best and most sustaining way to remember things is to get into the habit or routine of writing them down in one place (preferably a planner or agenda book) and looking in that place multiple times per day. This can be difficult at first, but just like brushing your teeth, once you do it enough it can become second nature. For the forgetful type, repetition and consistency is the key.

"Dug" the Dog—The Easily Distracted

If you were fortunate enough to see the fantastic 2009 award-winning Pixar film *Up,* you will surely remember the laughable, lovable character Dug the talking dog. Dug had a short attention span, to say the least. Every time he set forth on his journey and an errant noise or movement occurred, Dug completely lost his focus and shouted, "Squirrel!" It is no secret that being easily distracted is a major symptom of ADHD. What may not be as obvious is how distractibility plays into the idea of procrastination. Distractibility not only occurs in the moment, such as when one is briefly distracted by a noise, but it can also unravel even the best-laid plans when something else "comes up." To help control this impulse, "Dugs" must learn to set emotional boundaries within themselves in order to stay on task. The use of rewards and consequences for the completion of tasks can also aid in limiting attention as discussed in Chapter 2.

Heigh-Ho!—The Big Picture Type

Many adults with ADHD share the erroneous perception that most tasks come as an inseparable whole. By assuming that a particular goal or task cannot be subdivided or dealt with systematically, one can easily become overwhelmed and give up. In Chapter 5 on organizing your space, we discuss "chunking" in terms of space. The same principles can and should be used when it comes to both division of tasks and division of time. In Disney's *Snow White and the Seven Dwarfs*, the dwarfs kept their cottage in the woods dirty and disorganized. We believe this is because the dwarfs each looked at the huge mess and found it too much to handle. However, when Snow White broke down the space into seven small tasks that they could do individually, the place was cleaned up in no time.

Just as one space can always be divided into two smaller spaces, one task can always be divided into two smaller tasks. Just as one task can be divided into two smaller tasks, 1 hour can be divided into 2 half hours, and so on and so forth. Mastering this skill will ultimately reduce anxiety and feelings of being overwhelmed and, in turn, increase your motivation to continue a task to completion.

ABD—The Perfectionist

A small subset of adults with ADHD procrastinate because they have unusually high standards for themselves. Brownlow and Reasinger of Catawba College conducted a study in 2000 that examined the impact of motivation toward academic work and looked at what personality factors contribute to procrastination.[3] They found that perfectionism, among other factors, predicted procrastination in college students. In our offices, we occasionally see this type of client—a type we call "all but dissertation" (ABD). For example, Brad had been a stellar student, but he hit a roadblock halfway through his career when he was promoted to a managerial position. Finding himself in charge of other people, he became paralyzed and started to procrastinate on

---

[3]Brownlow, S., & Reasinger, R. D. (2000). Putting off until tomorrow what is better done today: Academic procrastination as a function of motivation toward college work. In J. R. Ferrari & T. A. Pychyl (Eds.), Procrastination: Current issues and new directions [Special issue]. *Journal of Social Behavior and Personality, 15,* 225–238.

assigning projects to his staff. The source of his procrastination was the incredibly high expectations he had created for himself over the years: getting straight *A*s and completing a master's degree straight out of undergraduate school. His managerial output became his personal "dissertation"; he did not want to produce a product that was anything less than spectacular, and therefore he did nothing. Just as Brad had to discover in treatment, the ABD individual must learn to create realistic goals—whether they involve writing a dissertation, planning a project, or even organizing the kitchen. Setting limits on the time allowed to complete a task and creating an effective incentive system will help you to gain control over your perfectionism.

My Procrastination Profile

Type(s): _____

_____

_____

_____

Example of a time I was the _____ type: _____

_____

_____

One thing I can do to procrastinate less in this way:

_____

_____

_____

Example of a time I was the _____ type: _____

_____

_____

My Procrastination Profile (*Continued*)

One thing I can do to procrastinate less in this way:

_____

_____

_____

Example of a time I was the _____ type: _____

_____

_____

One thing I can do to procrastinate less in this way:

_____

_____

_____

Example of a time I was the _____ type: _____

_____

_____

One thing I can do to procrastinate less in this way:

_____

_____

_____

HOW IS FEAR INVOLVED?

Fear-motivated procrastination typically expresses itself as avoidance and the powerful urge to either delay performing a task or wait for its expiration so that it no longer has to be dealt with. There are two types of fear in terms of task completion: fear of failure and fear of success. Former Swedish soccer manager Sven Goran Eriksson once said, "The greatest barrier to success is the fear of failure." He was half right. Fear of failure can render a perfectly capable person completely helpless and inoperative. The difference between successful people and unsuccessful people when it comes to fear is their view of feedback. Successful people take criticism as constructive. They accept that mistakes are going to be made, and they try to make fewer the next time. Unsuccessful people view criticism as personal rejection, a permanent fixture that prevents them from moving forward. If you allow fear to prevent you from completing tasks, the cluster of avoided tasks will increase over time. As outstanding tasks mount, you may become resigned, depressed, and immobile.

What Sven Goran Eriksson should have said is, "The greatest barriers to success are the fear of failure and the fear of success." Fear of success may seem silly to some, but it can be just as debilitating as a fear of failure. People commonly fear success because of how it may change them or their circumstances. Think of the phrase "It's lonely at the top." Success can be isolating. Success can also change others' expectations of you. You may believe that once you have shown a certain aptitude, you will be expected to perform at this level from then on. For example, if you put forth your best effort to complete a project at work on time and to perfection, sacrificing sleep and nutrition, will your boss expect you to do this for every project? If that is your belief, you may think it is better just to give a consistent mediocre performance.

If you think you may fall into one of these two categories, ask yourself, "What am I afraid of?" In fear-motivated procrastination, it is necessary to identify the fear to begin with. For example, an adult with ADHD who has struggled to find a job over an extended period of time may develop a fear of being rejected yet again. A college student with ADHD may put off completing her class project because of a fear of obtaining a high grade that her parents would expect her to repeat. A client named Joel had set a goal of taking time to assist his wife with the care of their children on weekends. For three weekends straight, Joel wrote in his planner to take the kids to the park from 12:00 to 4:00 on Saturday afternoons. For 3 weeks straight Joel returned to sessions admitting that he had instead watched football while his wife had watched the kids. After his counselor encouraged him to take a thoughtful look at why he was unable to complete this objective, Joel admitted, "I'm afraid that if I spend one Saturday with the kids my wife will enjoy her time off so much she'll want me to take them every Saturday, and I'll never watch another college football game again." If you believe you may have a deep-seated fear that is sabotaging your efforts to move forward, it may be best to talk to a trained therapist or counselor. If you are unwilling or unable to do so, the strategies in Part I on goal setting and using incentives may be able to help. Either way, sources of fear should be confronted before attempting the time-management, behavior-changing tools set forth in this book.

GETTING BACK ON TRACK: IMPROVING TIME MANAGEMENT

Now that we have discussed the reasons for procrastination, we can begin to integrate these ideas into a plan of action to help you overcome poor time management. Here are some ideas to help keep you on track.

Use kitchen timers, clocks, cell phones, computers, and calendars. These and other devices can break down time and issue alarms when a designated period of time has passed. The more external you make the passage of time and the more you structure that time with periodic physical reminders, the more likely you are to manage your time well.

Learn how to plan ahead realistically. Break down tasks or large goals into smaller, tangible objectives and provide these goals with appropriate deadlines. Breaking down a task into manageable subtasks or steps usually removes the threat and anxiety of having to do a large task all at once. Learn to break down tasks into 15-minute segments to begin with. As you get more practiced at it, you may be able to increase these blocks of time.

Keep a running list of "to dos" that you can enter into your schedule. Even items you perceive to be small, easy, or habitual should be kept track of. Check off the items as you go along.

Give yourself credit when a task is accomplished. For more on this idea, see Part I on goal setting and using incentives. By registering accomplishment tangibly, you will be more motivated to continue through your day.

Stay flexible and be prepared to change your plan. Things will inevitably come up to throw your perfectly outlined schedule off course, and you need to be able to adapt. Likewise, regardless of how effectively you manage your ADHD symptoms, you will occasionally have a "bad" day during which you are unable to complete the tasks at hand. We liken this situation to hiking up a mountain. You may get halfway up and hit a rough patch that causes you to stumble and lose your footing. When this happens, the important thing is not to then go rolling back down to the bottom of the hill. Instead, you should be able to brush yourself off, reroute your course, and find your way back up the trail. Finally, you may at some point become bored with a system that once worked very well for you—that's the nature of ADHD. Don't think this means you haven't found the "right" tool yet. It simply means that although that tool worked for a certain period of time (and may work again later), you need to find a new tool for a while.

Keeping these ideas in mind, the next step in managing your time more efficiently is to find a planner, appointment book, or software program that works for you. These tools help to address problems with disorganization as well as poor working memory. There is no "magic bullet" when it comes to agendas. Try not to get sucked into thinking you need some fancy or expensive device. In fact, deluxe planners that come with stickers, pockets, and categories for everything will probably make you feel more overwhelmed than you already do. Instead, think simple and straightforward to begin. Once you have the hang of using it, you can customize your planner to your liking. Next we discuss a few options for adults with ADHD and the pros and cons of each. In addition, we offer a way to enhance your time-management technique, regardless of what type of planner you choose.

Quarter-Hour Planners

We recommend that everyone try a quarter-hour planner first. This can be done via pencil and paper or online via programs like

Microsoft Outlook or Google Calendar. If you can master this type of time tracker, you have the best chances of keeping your days organized and efficient. What makes the quarter-hour planner unique is that it creates a visual representation of time in small segments. Most planners do not account for time, let alone 15-minute blocks of time. Instead, they provide you with a large empty rectangle that inside says "Monday." You are then expected to write down all the things you would like to get done that day and somehow fit it all into 24 hours. Quarter-hour planners, conversely, invite you to break down large tasks into smaller pieces and help you to see where you can fit a particular task into your busy day. For example, let's say it's Monday and you would like to cook a nice dinner from scratch for your family this coming Sunday. In the meantime you have to go to work, pay your bills, do laundry, clean yourself every day, and help children with homework (to name a few). You may think that on Sunday you can just make a quick trip to the grocery store and throw something on the table, but when you have tried this in the past you have ended up ordering take-out Chinese at the last minute because you "didn't have time." You do have time, and the quarter-hour planner will help you see where it is.

To use the quarter-hour planner effectively, you first need to list all of your ongoing weekly activities in order of priority, estimate the amount of time each will take, and insert those into your schedule. ADHD can cause an individual to concentrate mainly on the moment, taking focus away from the signals and internal sense that time is passing. Therefore, adults with ADHD tend to be poor estimators of how long a task may take or how

Help Yourself! Create a Quarter-Hour Schedule

First, create a list of your regular ongoing weekly activities and order them from most important to least important. On the adjacent line, write how long each task will take, remembering to err on the side of overestimation.

1. _____ _____
2. _____ _____
3. _____ _____
4. _____ _____
5. _____ _____
6. _____ _____
7. _____ _____
8. _____ _____
9. _____ _____
10. _____ _____
11. _____ _____
12. _____ _____
13. _____ _____
14. _____ _____
15. _____ _____
16. _____ _____
17. _____ _____
18. _____ _____
19. _____ _____
20. _____ _____

(continues)

Help Yourself! Create a Quarter-Hour Schedule (*Continued*)

Next, insert the previous items into the quarter-hour calendar week below, starting with the top-priority items and working your way down to the bottom of your list.

Time	Monday	Tuesday	Wednesday	Thursday	Friday
6:00 a.m.					
6:15 a.m.					
6:30 a.m.					
6:45 a.m.					
7:00 a.m.					
7:00 a.m.					
7:15 a.m.					
7:30 a.m.					
7:45 a.m.					
8:00 a.m.					
8:15 a.m.					
8:30 a.m.					
8:45 a.m.					
9:00 a.m.					
9:00 a.m.					
9:15 a.m.					
9:30 a.m.					
9:45 a.m.					
10:00 a.m.					
10:15 a.m.					
10:30 a.m.					
10:45 a.m.					
11:00 a.m.					
11:15 a.m.					

Help Yourself! Create a Quarter-Hour Schedule (*Continued*)

Time	Monday	Tuesday	Wednesday	Thursday	Friday
11:30 a.m.					
11:45 a.m.					
12:00 p.m.					
12:15 p.m.					
12:30 p.m.					
12:45 p.m.					
1:00 p.m.					
1:15 p.m.					
1:30 p.m.					
1:45 p.m.					
2:00 p.m.					
2:15 p.m.					
2:30 p.m.					
2:45 p.m.					
3:00 p.m.					
3:15 p.m.					
3:30 p.m.					
3:45 p.m.					
4:00 p.m.					
4:15 p.m.					
4:30 p.m.					
4:45 p.m.					
5:00 p.m.					
5:15 p.m.					
5:30 p.m.					
5:45 p.m.					
6:00 p.m.					

(*continues*)

Help Yourself! Create a Quarter-Hour Schedule *(Continued)*

Time	Monday	Tuesday	Wednesday	Thursday	Friday
6:15 p.m.					
6:30 p.m.					
6:45 p.m.					
7.00 p.m.					
7:15 p.m.					
7:30 p.m.					
7:45 p.m.					
8:00 p.m.					
8:15 p.m.					
8:30 p.m.					
8:45 p.m.					
9:00 p.m.					
9:15 p.m.					
9:30 p.m.					
9:45 p.m.					
10:00 p.m.					

Then, write down any "extra" activities you would like to schedule into your week:

a. _____

b. _____

c. _____

Help Yourself! Create a Quarter-Hour Schedule (*Continued*)

Break down the extra activities into small steps or segments of time. Write down the step and how long it will take:

a. _____

  I _____ _____

  II _____ _____

  III _____ _____

  IV _____ _____

  V _____ _____ Total Time: _____

b. _____

  I _____ _____

  II _____ _____

  III _____ _____

  IV _____ _____

  V _____ _____ Total Time: _____

c. _____

  I _____ _____

  II _____ _____

  III _____ _____

  IV _____ _____

  V _____ _____ Total Time: _____

Insert extra activities wherever you have space in your planner, ideally doing one small item per day or so.

much time has passed during a given task. Prior to creating a schedule, it is helpful to take a week or two to record what you did *after* doing it. This takes out the guesswork, providing a clear picture of how long each item on your list actually takes. We also advise that when in doubt, overestimate. As a general rule, adding an extra 15 and sometimes 30 minutes onto a given task can never hurt. Plus, you never know when you may need to run to the restroom.

For your work schedule you may choose to delineate work tasks within the same planner as your personal life, or use something completely different. Many people choose to use something like Microsoft Outlook if their entire office is on the same system, but then use a paper and pencil quarter-hour planner for everything else. If this is the case, you would need to simply draw a line through the hours you will need for work. And, don't forget this includes your commute! When listing weekly tasks, try to remember even the smallest of things such as brushing your teeth or taking out the garbage. They may seem insignificant, but these small events add up and if unaccounted for can cause major disruption to your schedule. The following is an example of just some of the things the average adult might include on his or her weekly schedule:

- At work (8 hours)
- Driving to work (45 minutes)
- Driving home from work (45 minutes)
- Sleep (7 hours)

- Shower and get ready for work (brush teeth, style hair, put on make-up, get dressed; 1.5 hours)
- Prepare and eat breakfast (30 minutes)
- Prepare lunch to bring to work (15 minutes)
- Have lunch (1 hour)
- Make dinner (30 minutes)
- Eat dinner (30 minutes)
- Get children up and off to school (45 minutes)
- Help children with homework (30 minutes)
- Take an evening walk (30 minutes)
- Take medication (15 minutes)
- Fold laundry (30 minutes)
- Vacuum the house (1 hour)
- Clean the bathrooms (30 minutes)
- Feed the pets breakfast (15 minutes)
- Feed the pets dinner (15 minutes)
- Water the plants (15 minutes)
- Get and go through the mail (15 minutes)
- Collect and take out the trash (15 minutes)
- Pay bills (30 minutes)
- Fill the car with gas (30 minutes)

Although it may seem a bit daunting to see so many items, remember that most adults with ADHD thrive with routine and structure. However, as mentioned in the study discussed earlier, some individuals will shy away from micromanaging (such as those with high anxiety) and will find this approach too nerve wracking. The only way to know is to try.

How to Prioritize

When deciding what tasks should come first, second, and third on your list, think of the consequences of not completing each task and whether there is a specific due date associated with each task. Use numbers, letters, or even colored star stickers to designate around five levels of priority, then create a legend to keep with your planner.

For example,

A. Task is "due" in 1 week or less, or my boss expects me to complete it ASAP. If not complete, I could lose my job.

B. Task is "due" in 2 weeks or less, or a team member has expressed that he would like to see results soon. If not completed, my coworkers will be angry.

C. Task is "due" in 3 weeks or more, or it is something that I would like to get off my plate. If not completed, I will be disappointed.

D. Task has no pending "due date" and is something that would be nice to have done at some point. If not completed, it's okay.

See p. 79 for a sample completed quarter-hour planner.

Once you have mastered the process of scheduling and following through with your regular schedule, you can attempt to insert some extra activities, such as the previous example of making a nice family dinner from scratch. To do this, first break down your goal of making dinner into smaller tasks or steps and estimate the time each will take, always overestimating by at least 15 minutes per task. Don't forget even the smallest of steps, such as setting the table before your meal.

JULY 25–31

WEEK 30

25 MONDAY WORK	**26** TUESDAY HOME	**27** WEDNESDAY WORK
7 — wake up	**7** — wake up	**7** — wake up
:15 exercise	:15 exercise	:15 exercise
:30	:30	:30
:45	:45	:45
8 breakfast & shower	**8** breakfast & shower	**8** breakfast & shower
:15	:15	:15
:30	:30	:30
:45 commute	:45 grocery store	:45
9 check email	**9** (remember list!)	**9** check email
:15	:15	:15
:30	:30 put groceries away	:30
:45 — break	:45 find recipe 4 tonite	:45 — break
10	**10** — break!	**10**
:15 staff meeting	:15	:15 staff meeting
:30	:30 vacuum 1st floor	:30
:45	:45	:45
11 project ABC	**11** — break!	**11** project ABC
:15 step 1	:15	:15 step 2
:30	:30 lunch	:30
:45 — clean up desk	:45	:45 — clean up desk
12 lunch	**12** vacuum 2nd floor	**12** lunch
:15	:15	:15
:30	:30 pay bills	:30
:45	:45	:45
1 — regroup!	**1** — break!	**1** — regroup!
:15	:15	:15
:30 phone call	:30 store - birthday gift	:30 plan project XYZ
:45	:45	:45
2 plan project XYZ	**2** prep food 4 dinner	**2** Project ABC step 3
:15	:15	:15
:30	:30	:30
:45 — break	:45	:45 — break
3	**3** — break!	**3**
:15	:15	:15
:30	:30 dust & bathrooms	:30
:45	:45	:45
4 check email	**4** cook dinner	**4** check email
:15	:15	:15
:30 prep for tomorrow	:30	:30 prep for tomorrow
:45	:45	:45
5 commute home	**5** — set table	**5** commute home
:15	:15 — clean kitchen	:15
:30	:30	:30
:45 walk dogs	:45 walk dogs	:45 walk dogs
6 heat & eat dinner	**6** eat dinner	**6** heat & eat dinner
:15	:15	:15
:30	:30	:30
:45	:45	:45
7 — clean kitchen	**7** — clean kitchen	**7** — clean kitchen
:15	:15	:15
:30	:30	:30
:45	:45	:45
8 RELAX!	**8** RELAX!	**8** RELAX!
:15	:15	:15
:30	:30	:30
:45	:45	:45

GOAL: Making Dinner for the Family

1. Find a recipe (30 minutes)
2. Write down necessary ingredients (30 minutes)
3. Drive to the store (30 minutes), buy groceries (2 hours), drive home (30 minutes), and unpack groceries (30 minutes; total: 3.5 hours)
4. Prep food (1 hour)
5. Cook food (1.5 hours)
6. Set the table (30 minutes)
7. Clean up the kitchen (1 hour)

Now you can clearly see how this task could take almost half a Sunday in itself, and if you left it to be completed all in one day, you would surely be disappointed. Because the rest of your schedule has been written out in the quarter-hour planner, you can now begin to insert these steps into the empty spaces throughout the week, leaving Sunday for Steps 5 through 7.

The most important thing when it comes to a portable planner such as the quarter-hour planner is to make its use a habit or routine. Make sure you carry it around with you, keep it in the same place when not in use (so that it doesn't get lost), and look at it several times a day, perhaps pairing this with your daily meals. However, as with all tools for adults with ADHD, quarter-hour planners have pros and cons.

Quarter-Hour Planner Pros:
- Creates a visual of time
- Allows you to break down large tasks into smaller subtasks

- Helps you to see where in your day a task may fit
- Creates structure and routine
- It is portable
- Minimizes tendency to become overwhelmed or procrastinate because tasks can be completed in small steps

Quarter-Hour Planner Cons:
- Micromanaging approach can increase anxiety for some
- Requires constant updating and weekly scheduling
- Must be opened and viewed several times a day

Large Monthly Calendars

Large monthly calendars offer some features that you won't find in most book-size, portable agendas. For starters, the paper versions are too large to move from place to place and therefore are harder to lose. Second, they allow you to see multiple weeks at a time rather than just one. When using a calendar that allows you to view one week at a time, it is difficult to keep long-term projects or upcoming events in mind. Often the scenario plays out like this: You are feeling confident because you have been regularly using your weekly agenda, writing in it, and checking it multiple times a day. You have a relaxing, carefree weekend. Then Monday comes. You sit down at your desk at 9:02 a.m., ready to face the day. You turn the page of your planner to your new week and—whoops! There, written in big capital letters is that big client meeting that was scheduled weeks ago. You completely forgot because there was no prep work other than to wear your best suit (which you did not) and psych yourself up (which you did not). Oh, and it started 2 minutes ago. Using a large monthly calendar may help you avoid this scenario. Whenever possible, we recommend using both a quarter-hour planner or other weekly agenda book in conjunction with a large monthly calendar.

We use the word *large* with intent—not just any monthly calendar will do. In order to most effectively plan long term with a monthly calendar, we suggest you purchase the paper version that is meant for a desktop. But do not put it on your desktop. If you do, it will surely get covered by stuff in no time. Instead, hang it on the wall next to your desk or wherever you do most of your work. The blocks on these desk calendars are large enough for you to write down multiple items. Many even come with lines within the box to help keep writing neat and organized. If you choose to use a computerized version like Google Calendar or Microsoft Outlook, set it to automatically pop up on starting your computer, and make sure you maximize the window to ensure you don't miss anything. With online systems, you can also set reminder alarms before big meetings, projects, and so forth.

Large monthly calendars are not meant for micromanaging. Leave nightly assignments and daily household tasks to the smaller weekly and daily planners. Instead, write only your large or long-term projects and big events on these time management tools. This will help you to keep a big picture view but not to the extent that you will become overwhelmed. Here are some pros and cons of a large monthly calendar.

Large Monthly Calendar Pros:

- Difficult to lose
- Can view multiple weeks at a time
- Large blocks fit lots of writing
- Helps you to see the "big picture"

Large Monthly Calendar Cons:

- Cannot write things as they come up—lack of portability with paper version
- Does not show time (only days)
- Not enough space for daily tasks/routine activities

 Color Coding

Many adults with ADHD consider themselves to be visual (learning through seeing) or kinesthetic (learning by doing) learners rather than auditory (hearing) learners. Verbal instructions often get forgotten about within minutes. All planners and agendas are visual aids to help you remember. The physical act of writing down what is to be done makes the practice of using a planner kinesthetic as well. Another highly effective way to strengthen the visual aspect of using a planner is color coding. Like any new tool, color coding takes some effort at first but ultimately can become routine and actually decrease your stress when engaging in time-management exercises. Take a look at the following list:

- Wash car
- Fix dinner

- Pay bills
- Answer e-mails
- Call boss
- Cancel credit card
- Mow the lawn

Seeing one big list can seem a little overwhelming, right? So instead, let's say that you have created a color-coding system that designates yellow for household chores, green for financial tasks, and red for work-related activities. The same list now looks like this:

- Wash car (yellow)
- Fix dinner (yellow)
- Mow the lawn (yellow)
- Pay bills (green)
- Cancel credit card (green)
- Answer e-mails (red)
- Call boss (red)

By using a color system, you have broken up what seemed like one blur of a list into three smaller, more manageable sublists. You can see priorities pop out easily—in this case using the color red for work-related activities may mean "Stop! Do these items first." Figure out a system that makes sense to you, using no more than four to seven colors to avoid confusion and negate the purpose of color coding. Once you have your system in place, color coding can be used in both weekly (quarter-hour) planners and large monthly calendars, as well as on the computer or with paper and highlighters.

High-Tech Time Management Devices

Mobile devices and PDAs have the benefit of being portable and accessible at the touch of a screen. However, because these devices are small, it is hard to get a complete picture on a tiny screen. Also because of their size, they are often lost or forgotten about inside a pocket or purse (or washing machine). Desktop or laptop computers pose the opposite dilemma; they are big enough and certainly noticeable, but their lack of portability and readiness makes adding tasks as they come difficult. A happy medium in the size versus portability dilemma can often be found in iPads or netbooks, which are both portable and feature a sizeable screen. Some adults with ADHD have great success with computer-based planning devices, and more and more ADHD-friendly technology is becoming available every day.

As mentioned previously, the most widely used and popular calendar systems include Google Calendar and Microsoft Office. These can be especially good choices if you need to merge your information with anyone else's, such as in an office setting. In addition, there are several ADHD-specific tools that are lesser known. For example, Skoach (http://www.skoach.com) is an online integrated task list and calendar with color coding and text-message and e-mail reminders that is accessible on most mobile devices. It was developed by clinical psychologist and ADHD authority, Kathleen Nadeau, specifically for adults with ADHD. Task Timer is an application that allows you to pick a task and choose the completion time. It helps to keep you on track by showing time elapsed and time remaining. It also includes breaks and uses a vibration reminder to help you stay on task. Epic Win uses video game elements to appeal to the ADHD brain. It incentivizes completing tasks by allowing you to pick up points and "treasure." The iReward Chart allows you to input goals and track progress over the course of a week and then earn stars on your way to completion of a task. You can find more information about time-management and to-do list tools on blogs and websites such as ADDitude (http://

Mobile apps for time management:

- Skoach
- Task Timer
- Epic Win
- iReward Chart

www.additudemag.com) and the Adult ADHD Success Network (http://www.adultaddsuccesstools.com).

If you choose to use a computer-based or online program to manage your time, it may be a good idea to have an old-fashioned backup for times when the system might fail. Used well, technology can be a great help to many adults with ADHD. Following are some pros and cons of advanced technology.

High-Tech Pros:
- Portability and accessibility of mobile devices and PDAs
- Can easily merge data with others
- Can set reminder alarms, group data, color code, etc.
- Online information can't get lost

High-Tech Cons:
- Lack of portability and accessibility of desktop and laptop devices
- Small size makes some devices easy to misplace or forget about

- Can't access data if the device isn't working or crashes
- Visually overstimulating or confusing to some adults with ADHD

No matter what system you choose, the most important factor will be to use it with diligence and consistency. The more routinely you use your preferred time-management tool, the easier and more mindless this task will become, freeing up your mental energy for more important things. Once you have mastered the art of time management, you will be well on your way to successfully managing many of your other ADHD symptoms.

SUMMARY

Here are the important points you will want to take away from this chapter. Use the following checklist to note the areas you have thoroughly studied. Leave the box empty if it is an area you would like to come back to and review further.

☐ I understand the pitfalls of time management as they relate to ADHD.

☐ I have discovered methods to combat struggles with time management.

☐ I can identify the reasons why I procrastinate and have learned how to resolve these issues.

☐ I have learned ways to reduce my fear as it relates to time management and getting things done.

☐ I understand how to get back on track when I slip up and have learned how to apply some specific time-management techniques.

CHAPTER FOUR

IMPROVING SOCIAL RELATIONSHIPS

If love is the answer, could you rephrase the question?
—Lily Tomlin

 One of the key tasks of adulthood is developing and maintaining social relationships. We begin as children learning about relationships from our parents, practice friendships throughout adolescence, and lay the groundwork for adult friendships and intimate relationships. Hopefully, we will find our "soul mate," commit to a long-term relationship, and enjoy the benefits of a lasting relationship with that person. We will also continue to maintain and nurture our friendships, as they will provide enjoyable times and emotional support throughout the ups and downs of our lives. The symptoms associated with adult ADHD can at times help a person to develop friendships but can also make long-term relationships a challenge. In this chapter, we discuss the ways that inattentiveness, hyperactivity, and distractibility can get in the way of your social relationships. Then, we discuss how executive functioning is important to relationships. We help you figure out if you are realistic in your self-perception of your social skills. The how-to part of this chapter gives you suggestions for paying attention in conversations and teaches you how to make a Listening Plan. We also give you a list of general tips to improve your social relationships. Start by taking the quiz to see if this is a chapter that will help you out.

QUIZ YOURSELF—DOES THIS SOUND LIKE YOU?

1. Do you blurt out things that you later regret?
2. Do you tend to interrupt others when having a conversation?
3. Do others complain that you don't listen or that you forget what they've told you?
4. Does your spouse or roommate complain that your space is always a mess?
5. Do you forget anniversaries and birthdays, or do you remember but can't quite seem to get a card or gift in time?
6. Do others complain because you are never on time for dates or planned activities?
7. Do you frequently lose your temper over something minor?
8. Are you accused of being self-centered, even though you don't think this is true of you?

WHAT THE EXPERTS SAY

Research has suggested that, beginning in childhood, those with ADHD have a difficult time with peer relationships. Children with symptoms of hyperactivity and impulsivity tend to show aggressive and disruptive behaviors. Their social skills, particularly when it comes to making friends, can be poorly developed. They seem to overwhelm other children by being excessively intrusive, abrupt, and inappropriate. Why do these behaviors occur? The reason is not clear, but some researchers think that children with symptoms of hyperactivity have a need to seek sensation. When there is no stimulation in the environment, they have a need to create some. As a result, they look for social disruption rather than smooth social interactions. Alternatively, children with more symptoms of inattentiveness tend to be more anxious and shy and to withdraw from others, which can lead to being neglected (as opposed to actively being rejected). Regardless of the symptoms, children with ADHD are more likely to be rated by peers as less popular, and they often rate themselves as feeling lonely.

Do these early social difficulties disappear? Somewhat, but not entirely. For example, Dr. Susan Young and her colleagues in England studied adults with ADHD and found them to have many more problems with friends than those without the disorder.[1] Dr. Kevin Murphy, who directs an ADHD clinic in Massachusetts, explained that adults with ADHD can have difficulties in understanding social cues and don't seem to attune their behavior to other people. Hence they can be perceived as rude or insensitive. They can also be described as moody and have frequent mood swings, often changing from happy to sad with little obvious provocation. Some partners

---

[1]Young, S., Gray, K., & Bramham, J. (2009). A phenomenological analysis of the experience of receiving a diagnosis and treatment of ADHD in adulthood: A partner's perspective. *Journal of Attention Disorders.* doi: 10.1177/1087054707311659

report that those with ADHD have very low frustration tolerance and tend to anger easily. There is a fairly high co-occurrence of depression with ADHD, which can be a strain on social relationships.[2]

Adults with ADHD tend to outgrow their symptoms of hyper-activity; however, the symptoms of inattention and impulsivity tend to remain and can be problematic. Research on ADHD and mar-riage has shown that the rates of getting married are not different for those with ADHD, but unfortunately, satisfaction with one's marriage tends to be lower. There is also evidence that separation and divorce rates are higher. One research study found that women were more likely to be supportive of male partners with ADHD and to be tolerant of their symptoms. Alternatively, men were more likely to divorce their spouse or leave the relationship when they were involved with a woman who had ADHD. Studies have shown that, in general, adults with ADHD feel that they get angry more easily, have temper outbursts, break up relationships over trivial matters, and have difficulties managing finances that lead to marital troubles. They also feel that they have a harder time keeping friend-ships. Why is this? Many relationship and marital problems can be related to what we know about ADHD.

Let's look at the three core symptoms of ADHD and see how each one of these can cause problems with different aspects of adult relationships. First, let's talk about *inattention.* Relationships are all about communicating, which generally revolves around having a

---

[2]Murphy, K. (2005). Psychosocial treatments for ADHD in teens and adults: A practice-friendly review. *Journal of Clinical Psychology, 61,* 607–619. doi: 10.1002/jclp.20123

conversation. Conversations require that you pay attention to the other person. If you have ADHD, you can usually do this for a short period of time or when the subject is really interesting, but when conversations are long, you may find you easily lose focus. It's kind of like listening to that biology lecture in school. There just seem to be other things going on in your head, and those other things can easily crowd out the other person's voice. This can cause that other person to get annoyed or frustrated with you and even accuse you of not paying attention on purpose, as if you had control over it. When we work with clients in treatment, we always ask about their social relations. Many clients admit that their friends or partners complain that they never listen. Many have actually been referred to us for exactly that reason. A boyfriend or girlfriend has gotten fed up and insists that they come to see us to help them learn how to pay attention.

Second, let's consider *hyperactivity*. Adults with ADHD do not display hyperactivity in the same obvious, "bouncing off the walls" way as children with the disorder. Still, individuals with ADHD often have a hard time with activities that require them to sit still or focus for long periods of time, even those activities that they enjoy. They may become restless and need to move from one activity to another fairly frequently. Their partners may interpret this as a sign that the individual with ADHD is bored with them or does not care enough to participate in an activity that's important to them. A common complaint might run along the lines of, "I went jogging with you yesterday when I didn't really feel like it. Can't you even sit through lunch with my friends without constantly checking your voicemail and then insisting you need to leave before I've even finished eating?" Sometimes, complaints turn into some variation of, "If you cared about me, you wouldn't act that way." Again, the other person seems to imply that you have control over your behavior and that if you cared about the relationship, you would just shape up!

Finally, *impulsivity* can be a strain on relationships. Do others complain that you talk too much and they can never get in a word edgewise? Do you sometimes say something that you think is funny or clever and realize later that it really hurt someone's feelings? Do you sometimes buy things on a whim or make decisions without really thinking them through? Does it seem like the expression "What was I thinking?" applies consistently and exclusively to you? These are symptoms of impulsivity and an inability to inhibit behaviors. There doesn't seem to be any lag or think time between the impulse and the action. An idea or behavior pops into your head, and before you consider it, it's been said or done.

Each of these difficulties can be traced back to the core symptoms of inattention, hyperactivity, and impulsivity. However, without realizing this, your partner or friends can misattribute the behaviors to not caring about the relationship, lack of consideration, or just not trying hard enough. They can become critical and blaming. This, in turn, causes you to try and justify your behavior. No one wants to feel bad, and trying to protect your self-esteem is a natural thing. So, you react by being resentful, blaming the other, and being unwilling to take responsibility for disagreements or problems. Do you see a vicious cycle here? Many times it's just easier to give up on the relationship and move on, without really learning from it.

If we look at the science, we can begin to understand how difficulties in relationships make perfect sense. As we've stated previously, adults with ADHD have difficulties in areas that are referred to as *executive function ing*. Executive functioning can be thought of as the primary control center in the brain that underlies most of our behaviors. Executive

Executive functioning "jobs":

- Problem solving
- Planning
- Short-term memory
- Inhibition
- Self-regulation
- Motor control

functions can be compared with managers in a large business. They plan and delegate activities to personnel throughout the organization who get the different jobs done. These "jobs" include key activities such as problem solving, planning, short-term memory, inhibition, self-regulation, and motor control. When one or more of these basic jobs are not being carried out, difficulties can occur. Remember the previous quiz? Did you respond "yes" to blurting things out or interrupting? These behaviors would fall under the realm of inhibition, self-regulation, and motor control. How about forgetting things? This would fall under short-term memory. The concept of executive functioning is still being investigated. The exact categories change between different studies, with some scientists including additional functions. Also, it's clear that not everyone with ADHD has deficits in all areas. One person with ADHD might have poor memory skills but be pretty good at inhibiting his or her motor impulsivity. Sometimes this depends on whether you have the predominantly inattentive type of ADHD or the predominantly hyperactive–impulsive type of ADHD.

However, executive functioning is a very important model in understanding ADHD and helps us explain how the "control center" in the brain can impact specific day-to-day behaviors that can have a tremendous impact on social relationships.

 WHY IS BEING REALISTIC SO DIFFICULT?

There's another mechanism called the *positive illusory bias* that has been studied in individuals with ADHD. The positive illusory bias is what happens when someone thinks they are better at doing something than is warranted by the evidence. For example, we frequently ask clients about driving a car. We ask them how many speeding tickets they've received, how many accidents they've been in, or if they've ever had their license taken away. We find that they are pretty good about answering these specific questions, which we call the *evidence*. Then we ask them to give an overall rating of how good a driver they are. We refer to this as their *self-description*. We frequently find that they rate themselves as a very good driver, even though the evidence they've just given us doesn't suggest that at all. We often find that the self-description is more positive than the evidence. We believe this type of responding is a characteristic of the positive illusory bias, in that they see themselves through rose-colored glasses. Research has supported this idea; those with ADHD are significantly more likely to give global self-ratings that are not supported by specific evidence. This can often happen in relationships. Adults with ADHD might really think that they are trying hard in a relationship, and so they are really blindsided when their partner criticizes them. Are they in denial, making things up, out of

touch with reality? We don't think
so. We think they really believe
what they are saying. Again, this
disconnect between the evidence
and the self-description seems to
be a by-product of the executive

> **Positive illusory bias:**
> Self-description that is
> more positive than what
> the evidence suggests.

functioning deficits, whereby those with ADHD just have difficulties with memory, sequencing, and logic. First, those with ADHD may not remember accurately what really happened or what they have done or said in the past. Second, they have a difficult time putting things in logical sequences. The result is a difficult time with self-appraisal.

Here's another example of the sequencing difficulty. Adults with ADHD are frequently late for appointments, meetings, or classes. When asked to give an estimate of how long it takes them to do something—for example, get to class—they will give an estimate that is really not enough time. They might estimate 30 minutes. But if they are asked to estimate separately how long it takes to fix and eat breakfast (15 minutes), shower (10 minutes), get dressed (10 minutes), drive to campus (10 minutes), look for parking (5 minutes), and walk into their classroom (5 minutes) and the minutes are added up, the total is almost an hour. Are they intentionally misstating the time? No, of course not. But their executive-functioning deficits make it difficult for them to break down the task and do that sequencing all at once. So they make a very global estimate that turns out to be inaccurate. Why does it seem to always be incorrect in the direction of underestimating time? Again, the reason is unclear. But there's a good chance that the positive illusory bias comes into play again, and they really want to believe that they are able to do things quickly. Some researchers think that individuals with ADHD have gotten so much negative feedback that they try to cope with this by seeing themselves in a more positive light whenever possible. This self-protective behavior can be very adaptive. But you can see how this can have an impact on social relationships. Go back to Question 6 at the beginning of the chapter. Did you check "yes"? This difficulty in sequencing, along with a positive illusory bias, might help explain why you are frequently late for dates or planned activities.

CAN YOU RELATE TO THIS?

The following case describes a young couple, David and Amanda. David was diagnosed with ADHD in the third grade and was now 30. He reported no trouble with making friends, but he admitted to some trouble keeping friends. He had dated several young women in college, and when he met Amanda he was immediately attracted to her. David sought help with depression when Amanda left him after a short but intense relationship.

David and Amanda had been dating for 5 months when Amanda told him that she wanted to break up. David was devastated by this announcement, as he thought their relationship was fine. He considered himself to be easy going, fun-loving, and kind. He was extroverted and loved to party. He was always up for an adventure, such as learning to scuba dive, going extreme mountain biking, skiing a black slope his first time out, or taking a road trip with his buddies on a moment's notice. David never had trouble finding friends to hang out with. He had dated several women, but when Amanda came along he was sure she was "the one." She had seemed immediately attracted to him, laughed at his zany humor, loved his sense of adventure, and told him he brought out the best in her. Amanda had confided that she was insecure about herself and couldn't quite believe that someone like David would be interested in her. David admired Amanda's stability. She kept him on track, kept him out of trouble, and was a wonderful listener. David had been making plans to buy her a ring.

After his initial confusion over Amanda's statement, David managed to sputter, "But our relationship is fantastic! How could you want to break up?" Amanda burst into tears and, between sobs, replied, "Of course, you think it's fantastic! Oh, David, you're clueless!" She started with a long list of complaints. David thought only about himself. He forgot everything she told him, even really important things like her best friend's engagement party that she had reminded him about five times. When he did remember to show up, he was always at least a half an hour late. It was like dating a 13-year-old. She was tired of having to remind him about everything. Amanda wanted to settle down and get married and have a family, but she couldn't imagine depending on David to do what adults were supposed to do. He was on his fourth job since college and was not really going anywhere, and Amanda wasn't sure he would be able to support her financially. He always got excited starting new things, but when the excitement wore off, his enthusiasm fizzled. At home, too, he would start numerous projects but never finish them. Amanda continued, "And you never pay any attention when I try to work on things!

I've told you how much it upsets me when you forget a date or are super late, and you always promise to do better. But it never lasts more than a week! Remember on Friday you promised to meet me for nachos and margaritas at Mexi's and you never showed up? I felt like such an idiot sitting there waiting on you! And you just forgot! Forgot! Like I don't mean anything to you!" David countered, "I didn't forget, I was biking and I really thought I'd be back earlier and I didn't have my phone with me." Amanda jumped in, "How many times have I asked you to bring your phone when you bike?" As Amanda continued, David felt himself slipping away, he couldn't focus on all this right now, and so he tried to listen to her while thinking that he needed to call Sam and see if he wanted to go kayaking. Miraculously, David's phone rang right at that moment and he answered it quickly. It was one of the guys from work. David listened a minute, barely registering as Amanda stormed out of the room. When he was finished with the phone call, he thought about going after her but decided it would be useless. He would just mess things up and make it worse. Besides, she was being ridiculously unfair. Instead, he called his buddy Sam and suggested they go out; anywhere was fine with David. He would deal with Amanda later.

David went to a bar with Sam, initially in a horrible mood. Over a few beers, he told Sam about Amanda's blowup, emphasizing how unreasonable Amanda was. Sam agreed. David felt much better, and by the time they left the bar, he had pretty much returned to his normal cheerful state. He was especially busy the following day but called Amanda immediately on waking the day after and suggested that they hang out that evening. Amanda was cool and remote. David sensed that the conversation was not going well but proceeded to tell Amanda a long story about a funny incident with one of his roommates that he was sure would make her laugh. Amanda was not amused, and in fact, there was a long silence at the place where he expected her to laugh. "What's wrong?" he asked. "Are you still upset about the

> **Common social traits of adults with ADHD:**
>
> • Outgoing
> • Friendly
> • Adventurous
> • Fun-loving
> • Kind

other day?" Amanda retorted that she had expected him to at least call her the day before when he knew how upset she was. She couldn't believe that he had gone drinking instead, but of course, she retorted, that was just like him. She was clearly angry, and David felt himself losing control in return. He was calling her and trying to be pleasant, so what more did she want? He was doing all the work here; maybe it just wasn't worth it. He was no good at relationships, and he always screwed them up. He was tired of constantly being criticized and nagged. He never got credit for the good things he did. Why bother trying to fix it?

This scenario illustrates many issues seen in the adult social relationships of individuals with ADHD. David has many positive traits and finds it fairly easy to make friends. His friendliness and outgoing nature are wonderful attributes. He is adventuresome and meets lots of new people through his many activities. He has dated quite a bit, and each new relationship starts out well. However, similar patterns soon emerge. David's girlfriends have common complaints: lack of attention, inability to finish things or taking an inordinately long time, forgetfulness, and chronic lateness. His communication skills are poorly developed, especially when it comes to conflict and resolving arguments. Because things are not generally resolved, old arguments simmer, just below the surface, and erupt easily. Arguments become more and more common, and David finds ways to escape, such as avoidance or drinking with his buddies. Almost all of his relationships end with his girlfriend leaving him. It is invariably a tearful parting, with the girlfriend claiming to love him but just not being able to put up with his many issues. David never really understands how to make things better but always manages to find another relationship.

Take a look at the executive-functioning tasks described previously. You should be able to see how many of these can be involved in the difficulties David is experiencing. Smoothly running control centers for problem solving, planning, short-term memory, inhibition, and self-regulation would have helped David tremendously as he attempted to respond to some of Amanda's needs. So let's take a look next at how we can use some of those skills in a critical area of relationships.

 ## GETTING BACK ON TRACK: BETTER COMMUNICATION SKILLS

Communication is a key to building good relationships. It is the foundation for getting to know someone, sharing experiences, and establishing the rules for how you will relate to one another. When you first meet someone, you quickly learn enough about the other to decide whether things will "click" and whether this is someone you might want to be friends with. How does that happen? How do you decide that some people are worth pursuing as friends and others are not? Think about your current friends. Think back to when you first met them and what led to your becoming friends with them. Maybe it was shared interests or merely being in the same situation at the same time. Maybe it was sports, college, a job, church, a club, or activity, or maybe you just met through common acquaintances. What was your common link? Did you actively decide that you wanted to pursue this person as a friend, or did you just drift into a relationship? No matter what the circumstances, your ability to communicate likely had an impact on your continuing relationship.

TRY IT! PAYING ATTENTION IN CONVERSATIONS

Think about the types of things you need to communicate with your partner or friends. Possibilities include household chores, social events, day-to-day activities in your life, gossip, or feelings. You may also need to learn how to do damage control when you've upset someone. When you have conversations, try to think about your communication style. Most people can classify themselves generally as a talker or a listener. Many times, individuals with ADHD are accused of talking too much and not paying attention. So let's focus on the skill of paying attention.

Step 1: Identify and Gather Evidence About the Issue

First, let's just think about communication in general for a minute and divide this up into its positive and negative components. The positive aspect of your communication style might be that you are entertaining, funny, enjoyable to be around, perhaps even the life of the party. You may be good at telling stories, very creative and dramatic, and have a great sense of fun and adventure. People may be attracted to you and enjoy being around you. But do you ever get the sense that you are alone in the midst of people? Do you sometimes feel that your relationships are superficial? There may be a negative aspect of your outgoing personality. You might be neglecting to let others talk and not paying attention to the needs of others, and so your relationships might be a bit one-sided.

So, as a first step, let's gather some evidence. Pick two or three situations during the coming week. Have "normal" conversations. Don't do anything different except try to reflect on the conversations once you've finished. Each time, after the conversation is over, think about the definition of *positive listening* below and rank yourself on a scale of 1 to 5. Here is the definition of positive listening:

> I paid attention. I can repeat specifics of the conversation. I remember specific things the other person asked me to do. I remember details, times, and dates of any plans made. I listened as much as I talked. I focused. My mind didn't drift. I learned something about the other person such as something they did, how they felt, or something they want me to do. I think this conversation deepened my relationship with this person.

Now give yourself a 1-to-5 rating for positive listening, as follows, for how you listened in general, across the 2 to 3 conversations you monitored.

I think that, in general, I listened:

1	2	3	4	5
Not at all	Somewhat	Pretty Good		Really Well

Now, let's try getting some outside confirmation. Think about your key relationships. Perhaps check out your rating by asking at least one other person to do the rating of you as well. You may not realize how your listening skills come across to others. Is your rating the same as the other person's? Go back and read the definition of positive listening. What specific parts of the definition tend to be challenges for you? What parts do you think you do pretty well?

Step 2: Commit to Change

Using your previous data gathering, think about whether this is an area you want to change. The more you think you need to change, are motivated to change, and commit to wanting to change, the easier and more successful you will be. Did you or your friend identify any specific areas that might be a problem? Think of examples of how not paying attention in conversations might have gotten you in trouble with friends. Visualize a different you. How would that look? This can be part of your motivation to change. Would it make your life better? Would it improve your relationships? Would it improve how you think about yourself? What positive things might happen to your relationships if you became a better listener? Are there situations in which you do attend that have turned out well?

After thinking through these questions, make a commitment to changing your listening behavior. Write down some specific things you want to accomplish. Some can be very specific; others can be a little more general. Here are some examples:

- I want to remember appointments and plans I've made with my husband.
- I want my friends to know I care about their problems.
- I want my friends to think I'm a good listener.
- I don't want to have to be reminded again and again of things people tell me.

Write your intended accomplishments in the space below. Prioritize them. Put the most important one first, as you are going to work on them one at a time:

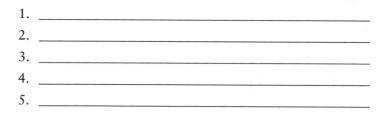

1. _____
2. _____
3. _____
4. _____
5. _____

By writing these down, you have established a commitment to change. If you're like many individuals with ADHD, the how-to is not usually the biggest obstacle. You're probably pretty bright, and it's probably pretty easy for you to identify areas and know that change is needed. It's the motivation part that can be difficult. That's why Step 2 of this exercise is so important. You're probably used to people telling you what your problems are and how to fix them. You probably have lots of experience with parents or teachers giving you direction and being in charge of your "personality makeover." But unless you take charge of the things you want to change, it will always be someone else's responsibility, and you will just be the one who's taking orders. By making up the orders and giving them to yourself, your motivation to change will increase dramatically.

Step 3: Make a Listening Plan

Let's start with the first item on your Listening Goals. First, you need to decide the best method for you to describe, chart, and remember your plan. You might choose to write it on a piece of paper and tape it to your bathroom mirror, you might write it on a whiteboard on your refrigerator, you might put it in a notebook that you review daily, or you might keep it on a notes program in your laptop or phone. The only requirement is that you write it somewhere that can be reviewed daily. We'll do a sample here, and you can model yours after that. For the sample, we're going to choose the goal, "I want to remember appointments and plans I've made with my wife." We're going to write the goal at the top of a piece of paper, and the paper is going to go on the bathroom mirror. Look at the sample Listening Plan provided in this chapter and fill in your own goal on your own plan.

Next, we'll fill in a 1-week objective. This should be something we can accomplish in a 1-week time frame that relates to our overall goal. For our first attempt, it should be something we really think we can accomplish. We want to start fairly easily so we don't get discouraged right off the bat. Our 1-week objective will be, "I want to remember one important activity I've planned with my wife, and stick to it." Choose your 1-week objective and write it down. It should be something that leads directly to your overall goal. Sometimes your overall goal can be accomplished in a single week, so the goal and the 1-week objective will be the same thing. But usually it will take more than a single 1-week objective to reach your goal.

Next, we'll fill in some short-term or daily objectives. These are the steps we need to take during the week that will lead up to the 1-week objective. Try to make them very specific, with each of them a specific behavior. For example, we have four: writing down our activity and putting it in our planner, checking it daily, confirming the activity the day before, and setting a reminder alarm.

Finally, we'll put in some rewards and consequences. These are really important, so don't skimp here. If you have ADHD, you can come up with the goal and the behaviors easily. It's the follow-through that gets you in trouble. You need to be motivated—so, let's digress just a moment and review some ideas from Chapter 2 on motivation before we finish our Listening Plan.

Here, we will expand on the idea of motivation, as presented in Chapter 2, and explain how it relates to relationships.

Motivation can be defined as an internal state or condition that energizes someone to engage in a behavior. The source of the motivation can be either external (I'll do this job so I'll receive a paycheck on Friday) or internal (I'll play the piano because I love the way it relaxes me). Motivation can also be described as positive, somewhat like a reward (the paycheck), or negative, such as avoiding a punishment (I'll drive the speed limit so I don't get a speeding ticket).

Research has shown that those with ADHD exhibit very different motivational styles. They tend to need more immediate motivation, and they seem to have a harder time creating internal motivation. Repetitive tasks are espe-

> **Motivation:** An internal state or condition that energizes someone to engage in a behavior.

cially difficult without motivation, and individuals with ADHD are more likely to just stop or quit a task. Some scientists have concluded that those with ADHD have poorer general ability or cognitive skills than those without ADHD. But this is not entirely true. Many times, if the scientists actually measure the motivational level of participants in these studies, they tend to find that it's the lack of motivation, rather than the lack of ability, that sets the ADHD participants apart from the non-ADHD participants. Why is this? Think back to the previous discussion on executive functioning. Motivation requires good short-term memory to keep in mind what the reward will be, it requires the ability to bridge delays and not lose focus, it requires attention to the task at hand, and it requires an internal self-talk that helps to regulate one's behavior. All of these capabilities can be affected by executive-functioning deficits. So the end result is that you have a very difficult time with self-motivation. You know how to do a task; you just can't manage the follow-through.

If you think back to when you were in elementary or high school, you can probably remember times when parents or teachers served as your external motivators. Perhaps you were involved in a reward system in which you received points and then specific rewards for completing tasks—constantly reminded to complete your homework. Or maybe you were forced to study on a particular schedule or required to take assignment check-off sheets back and forth between home and school. Did you feel like you frequently had a parent or teacher looking over your shoulder and prodding (or perhaps nagging) you to do things? If so, you probably got used to this kind of external motivation (both to gain positive rewards and to avoid negative consequences). When you went away to college or lived on your own for the first time, did you have a difficult time providing that motivation for yourself? It probably felt great at first to be in charge of your own life, but you probably realized at some point that self-motivation is a tough thing for individuals with ADHD. Let's get back to our Listening Plan and work on providing the motivation you need to complete the plan.

Look at the Motivation section of the sample Listening Plan. You'll see five different motivators listed there. Notice that some are internal and some are external. You'll also notice that some are positive and some involve avoiding negative consequences. You'll need to experiment to see what types work best for you. The motivation that might work best for other people may have no effect on you. Some people reward themselves with money, shopping, watching TV, food, naps, exercise, trips, going out, checking Facebook, or just spending time on the Internet. Others do things just because they know they will feel a sense of satisfaction from having done something well or correctly, but this may be difficult for you as an adult with ADHD. Finally, there are many negative reinforcements, many of which involve not disappointing someone else. It can be helpful to write several motivators on your plan so that if one doesn't work, the others might. Look back over them and see if you can identify them as internal and external. Also try to identify positive rewards versus avoidance of negative consequences. Did you seem to have a preference for one particular type? It may be helpful to use your list of rewards and consequences from Chapter 2. Try the plan for a week.

Sample Listening Plan

Goal
Goal 1: I want to remember appointments and plans I've made with my wife.

1-Week Objective
1-Week Objective: I want to remember one important activity I've planned with my wife and stick to it.

Short-Term Objectives
Short-Term Objective A: I want to write down our activity in my appointment book.
Short-Term Objective B: I want to review my appointment book every night right before I go to bed.
Short-Term Objective C: I want to review the activity with my wife the day before, and let her know I've remembered it.
Short-Term Objective D: The day of our activity, I want to put a reminder in my cell phone, and have it beep me 10 minutes before I need to start.

Motivation
1. My wife will be happy with me (external positive result).
2. I'll feel better about myself (internal positive result).
3. I'll also reward myself by setting aside $10 and spending it on anything I want if I meet my one week goal (external positive result).

(continues)

Sample Listening Plan (*Continued*)

4. I'll punish myself by not watching *American Idol* on TV next week if I don't follow through on my plan (external negative result).
5. My wife and I will get in an argument if I don't follow through (external negative result).

Modify Plan

I forgot the planned activity with my wife. I reviewed this list to see which thing went wrong. I put the activity in my calendar, but then didn't check it or do anything else on the plan. I bought her flowers, apologized, and showed her my plan to let her know I'm trying. I'm doing the same plan next week, but this time I'm putting a big reminder on my laptop that says, LOOK AT YOUR CALENDAR BEFORE YOU CHECK E-MAIL. I'm also changing my rewards and putting in some more external rewards.

 Step 4: Evaluate and Modify

How did the plan work? If you were successful, what things seemed to make it work? Build on those things and proceed to your second goal, filling in all the steps the same way you did for your first goal. If you were not successful, what were the obstacles? Was the goal too difficult to expect immediate success? What do you need to change? The objectives? The motivators? Don't give up. Think this through, talk to the person or persons involved in the plan, and see if you can get some feedback from them. They might have a very different perspective than you. Modify and redo the plan, and try it for another week. Just working on the plan, whether or not you are immediately successful, will help you to think through your behaviors. Remember, this is under your control, and just the process of going through the steps can help train your mind to eventually do this more naturally. Ultimately, you want to reach the place where you're doing automatically what mom or teachers did for you in terms of making plans and encouraging you to be motivated. That's what self-regulation is all about. And by letting important people in your life know that you are taking active steps to improve your relationships, they will perceive you differently. They might let go of that misperception that you don't care or you're not willing to change.

After reading this chapter, you might want to do some additional work on your own. The tips that follow can be helpful as easy reminders.

TRY IT! TIPS FOR IMPROVING SOCIAL RELATIONSHIPS

- Make a list of your positive traits. There are lots of reasons why others like you. Focus on those!
- When talking, look the other person directly in the eye. It will help you to focus on what he or she is saying.
- Practice repeating back what someone has just said to you in a conversation ("So you're worried that you might be fired because the boss is jealous of your skills?"). This will help you focus on the conversation, remember what's important to the other person, and let that person know you are listening.

- Pay attention to body language. Get used to guessing what someone is "saying" when they blink, cross their legs, tighten their lips, fold their arms, laugh nervously, look away, squint, or suddenly quit talking.

- Try to stop what you're doing when someone starts talking to you. Don't look at the computer, read the paper, or watch TV while trying to have a conversation.

- Make a conscious effort to stop talking regularly in a conversation and let the other person have a turn. Learn to ask questions to draw the other person out.

- Try to look for natural pauses in a conversation before you jump in. At the very least, wait until the end of the sentence.

- Avoid making major decisions without doing at least one of the following: wait overnight, make a list of pros and cons, or check out your plan with someone else.

- When you start a household task and think you're finished, ask yourself, "Am I really done? Did I put away my stuff? Clean up after myself? Put things back where they belong?"

- Always try to write down appointments, dates, anniversaries, meetings, and tasks in one common place and check this daily.

- When figuring out how long it will take you to get somewhere, avoid being late by breaking down your estimate into pieces (getting ready, driving, stopping for gas, parking).

- Be aware that your partner/spouse/friends can't read your mind. Tell them specifically what you want or need or mean.

- Do nice things for the important people in your life.

- Frequently remind yourself of your spouse's or partner's positive qualities. Either write them down in a journal or actually tell the person.
- Develop interests and passions. You'll be much more enjoyable in a relationship if you like your life and don't depend on your partner to make you happy.

SUMMARY

Here are the important points you will want to take away from this chapter. Use the following checklist to note the areas you have thoroughly studied. Leave the box empty if it is an area you would like to come back to and review further.

☐ I understand the areas of difficulty in my social relationships and how ADHD impacts my social behavior.

☐ I can appreciate how the positive illusory bias might help explain why I am not always realistic or accurate in my self-appraisals.

☐ I have practiced positive listening and paying attention.

☐ I have learned many brief tips that can be especially helpful in improving social relationships.

CHAPTER FIVE

ORGANIZING YOUR SPACE

Organized people are just too lazy to look for things.
—Bertrand Russell

 Chronic disorganization is a cornerstone symptom of ADHD. Important papers and items often get lost beneath piles of clutter. Eventually these piles become closets and rooms full of stuff, both needed and unneeded. Forget finding that perfect dress to wear on your night out; you'd probably be happy with clean underwear most days. Then, on those days when you feel a little more motivated, you may even begin to weed through it all. However, more often than not you eventually become overwhelmed and give up or get distracted by all the cool stuff you are finding along the way.

This chapter will help you to begin to organize your environment in a way that makes sense to you as an adult with ADHD. To help you to get organized, we present reasons or motivating factors for becoming more organized; strategies for the before, during, and after stages of organization; a case example of one of our clients who struggled in this area; and some fill-in exercises to help you create and implement your own plan. Start by taking the quiz to see if this chapter will be helpful to you.

QUIZ YOURSELF—DOES THIS SOUND LIKE YOU?

1. Are you constantly losing or misplacing everyday items such as your keys, cell phone, iPod, or wallet?
2. Do you forget what color your desktop or kitchen table are because they are constantly covered in clutter?
3. Is your briefcase or backpack full of crumpled bits of paper, candy wrappers, and possibly those lost keys?
4. Do you insist something was never given to you, only to find it weeks or months later?
5. Do your closets look "like a bomb went off"?
6. Do you start to organize your home only to become overwhelmed and/or distracted?

WHAT THE EXPERTS SAY

Deficits in particular areas of the brain explain the symptoms of ADHD, including why it is so difficult for a person with ADHD to organize. Executive functions direct an individual's thoughts and actions, and these functions do not operate efficiently for adults with ADHD, leading to the classic symptoms of inattention, hyperactivity, and impulsivity. Let's take a look at each of these symptoms in relation to organization.

In terms of inattention, differences in your adult ADHD brain make it difficult to filter unwanted information and focus on only that which is necessary to get the job done. The result is chaos in the form of scattered thoughts and scattered stuff. This inability to filter and focus leads to chronic disorganization in many ways. First, when new things are brought into the home, getting distracted can affect where items are put. In addition, existing items are often misplaced. Next, a vicious cycle ensues because added clutter increases information to the environment, and there is more to filter. Finally, trouble focusing and filtering makes the idea of creating and following through on an organization plan seem as impossible as climbing Mount Everest.

Hyperactivity and impulsivity cause further issues in relation to organization. Hyperactivity may make it difficult for you to sit still and attend to many activities, especially those that you find boring or that require concentration. We would wager a guess that a lot of people, even those without ADHD, find organizing pretty boring. Furthermore, impulsivity makes it difficult to stay on task when other, more interesting things are going on, distracting you from your well-meaning effort to organize. Attempting to weed through piles of stuff, especially when you aren't sure what you are going to uncover, can lead to many distractions throughout the process. Going through a box of old clothes only to discover your 10th grade diary? Forget it. Not to mention that the "boring" task of organizing is usually in competition with ringing phones, TV shows, or screaming children.

More often than not, adults with ADHD can be their own worst enemies—creating chaotic spaces that serve to increase their inner turmoil. The core symptoms of ADHD all affect your ability to conquer the task of organizing in different ways. However, there are several coping skills that can be developed to overcome these challenges, which will be discussed below. Moreover, there are many advantages to becoming more organized that you may or may not realize. First and foremost, freeing up space gives you more of it, and not just physically but mentally and emotionally—less material clutter equals a less cluttered mind. Also by creating and sticking to rules of organization, you will have more free time to spend doing the things you really want to, with the people you want to be with. By putting in a little time up front, you will ultimately save more time in the long run. Organization rules that become routine will also contribute to reducing mental fatigue and making you feel less overwhelmed, because you won't have to think hard to decide where something should go. Less stuff also means less dust and fewer allergens, so you may literally become healthier by breathing in fewer environmental toxins. You will be a good role model to your spouse, kids, and friends, which let's face it, just feels good. Looking around at your clean space will feel good too, providing you with a dose of self-esteem and accomplishment every day when you walk through the door.

To make the process of creating and maintaining organization as underwhelming and streamlined as possible, we will break it down into the following three steps: Before, During, and After.

BEFORE GETTING ORGANIZED

We know it can be daunting for you, as an adult with ADHD, to even begin to think about getting organized. In an effort at self-

Why Get Organized?

✓ Less material clutter = Less mental clutter

✓ More time to spend doing things I enjoy

✓ I will feel less overwhelmed knowing where things belong

✓ My health may improve

✓ I will be a good role model to my family and friends

✓ I will enjoy coming home and seeing what I have accomplished

preservation, individuals sometimes say that they prefer living in clutter and chaos. We suspect that in most cases this statement is untrue, knowing the havoc clutter and chaos typically create for adults with ADHD, as well as the positive benefits created from an organized space. Instead, statements such as these usually come from a place of fear: fear of failure, fear of embarrassment, even fear of success and the expectations that accompany it. These fears come in the form of self-doubting questions such as, "What if I can't follow through and complete my organization needs?," "What will people think of me if they know how disorganized I really am?," or "How will I ever keep things organized once everything is cleaned up?" These fears need to be challenged. We suggest writing each one down. Then, write a corresponding "challenge thought" that discounts each fear. These are optimistic and realistic, glass-half-full ideas that serve to "beat up" on your doubts: "If I create and follow a step-by-step plan and take my time, I will complete my organization needs eventually" or "No matter how disorganized and cluttered my house is, there are worse houses out there." (If you need convincing of that

Challenge thoughts:
Optimistic and realistic, glass half-full ideas that "beat up" on your doubts.

one, turn on the A&E channel and watch an episode of "Hoarders.") Another challenge thought might be, "By instilling new rules and routines I will be able to stay organized with relative ease."

For adults with ADHD, this innately difficult ability to organize often gets further complicated by the idea that things need to be "perfect." Let go of this idea now. As the old adage goes, it's progress—not perfection. Your goal in terms of organization should be to create and maintain a system for simplifying your space that you can manage with relative ease. In addition to the idea of improving rather than perfecting your ability to organize, it is important to approach the task of organizing in a realistic way. Large projects like cleaning out the basement should not be attempted in a day or you are bound to disappoint yourself. Therefore, time management is closely tied to organization. In a sense, it is just another form of organization—organizing *time*. Review Chapter 3 for specific ideas for time management. The ideas presented there should be used in conjunction with those set forth in this section. In this chapter, we focus on organization in terms of organizing stuff or things— physically creating a simplified space to live and work, thus reducing the chaos and added stress that a messy environment generates.

The following is a checklist of things you should do prior to organizing your space. Make sure you complete the list for each new undertaking. Remember, the more planning and preparation you do, the less time you will need for the task and the less stress you will experience.

1. Relinquish your fears. Write them all down. For each one, write a corresponding "challenge thought." Think about what you might tell a friend who expressed such a concern.

2. Think in terms of improving the organization of your space, not perfecting it. Keep a note with the phrase "Progress Not Perfection" taped to the wall as you work.

3. Resist the urge to try to organize everything at once. It has been there this long; what's the harm in it being there a bit longer? Use a planner and a timer to keep to small chunks of time.

4. Create a list of the areas you would like to organize and then number them from the most important to least important areas. Complete one project at a time.

5. Decide on how you will organize each space before diving in.

6. Figure out what motivates you to organize your space. If organization in and of itself is not motivating to you (which it most likely is not), create another incentive. Maybe you will sell old items for money. Maybe you are creating a fun area where your kids can play or you just want to see the look on your boss's face. Review Chapter 2 on setting goals using rewards and consequences for more ideas about motivational strategies.

DURING GETTING ORGANIZED

In this section, we present various tips for organizing all of your stuff, from everyday usage items like keys, wallets, and mail to important papers about upcoming work projects. The suggestions are general and apply to most people with ADHD. If you need help deciding on specific labels for your filing system (as in, "Should I file my bills by date or by category?"), don't hesitate to get the opinion of a friend, family member, ADHD coach, or professional organizer. What system ultimately works for you is based on personal preference, and there is no magic bullet. According to feedback from our clients, the following strategies tend to work for many adults with ADHD.

Keep, Throw, or Donate

As you begin to weed through the items in your home or office, label each item for one of three categories: *Keep, Throw,* or *Donate.* There are a few ways you can do this. For small items, piles will work. Lay down three different blankets, one for each category, and place your items on the appropriate blanket. For larger items, try a color-coding system. A former client, Ryan, decided it was time he cleaned out his basement, which was full of everything from old furniture to children's toys. To distinguish the items among the three categories, he purchased an inexpensive pack of circular stickers of varying bright colors at an office supply store. As he decided where each item belonged, all he had to do was adhere the corresponding sticker to the item and move on. Although Ryan loved this idea and how it helped to streamline the organizing process for him, he discovered another issue in need of resolution. Each item was filled with a memory, and he struggled with whether to part with many of them. He even stumbled across an old journal and ended up spending an hour reading through it. To over-

come this dilemma, Ryan agreed
on a time limit to decide where
each item went. He set his watch
timer for 2 minutes per item. If

Try it out: Keep, throw,
or donate.

he had not decided by the time his alarm rang, the item went into
the trash.

For the items you choose to keep, there is another decision to
be made: Does the item get placed in a spot for everyday use, or does
it go into storage? Take into account how often you have used the
item in the past 6 months and how likely it is to be used in the next
6 months. If the answer is only a few times or less, storage may be
your best bet. And no, on top of your kitchen table is not a storage
area. Designate a particular part of the basement, garage, or closet
for storage and group like items together. Place items in large and,
more important, clear plastic bins so that you can easily find things
when you need them. And don't forget to label!

In summary, the keep, throw, or donate rule works like this:

1. Decide a way to identify items for each category. For
   smaller items, place them on blankets. For larger items, use
   a sticker system.
2. Plan to organize for short periods of time (30 minutes or
   less) and take frequent (10 minute) breaks.
3. Set a timer for approximately 1 to 3 minutes per item. If
   you have not decided where the item belongs when the
   alarm sounds, it goes into the trash.
4. Once you have divided all of your items, remove your
   throw and donate items as soon as possible.

5. For keep items, decide whether you want to store them or find an everyday space for each item. Use the same rules you applied for the first round (create a labeling system, organize for short periods of time, and set a timer to decide quickly).

6. Designate a suitable area of the home or office for storage items. Use clear containers to store items and label appropriately.

Divide and Conquer

After Ryan made the decision to organize his basement, he struggled to know where to start. When attacking a larger space such as an entire room, it is helpful to first divide it into areas and treat each area as a separate smaller space to be organized. Together we talked about the layout of his room and a logical breakdown of areas. In Ryan's case, his basement consisted of a living area that included a large closet and a set of bookshelves, as well as a bar that had become additional storage space. This gave us four spaces to divide and conquer: the open floor space in the living area, the closet, the bookshelves, and the bar. Because the closet was large, we further divided it into segments: the floor, hanging items, and the upper shelf. Before you begin to attack any space, take a look at it. Do you get overwhelmed by where to begin? If so, break it down until each segment is small enough to tackle. If you break the area into four smaller areas and it still seems overwhelming, break them down again. You may need to create 10 two-by-two foot spaces before you feel ready to begin. That's okay. As you conquer each small space, your confidence will grow and each new area will become easier to handle.

Alternatively, if you cannot come up with a logical division of your space (e.g., you are tackling a child's playroom that is covered in toys from top to bottom), divide the space like a grid. Create four quarters using brightly colored string, and organize each quarter one at a time. A similar idea can be used when tackling organization on your home or work computer. How about going through and deleting old files from one folder a day? Or, maybe use a "hard drive, flash drive, or recycling bin" rule. Regardless of which method you choose, or whether in the real or virtual world, list your segments from easiest to most difficult and always attack the easiest first.

Photographs

One novel and creative idea suggested by a former client is the use of photographs when dealing with organizational goals. Jenny developed a goal of organizing her home office and created several weekly objectives, including cleaning her workspace and setting up three separate filing systems. On her own accord, Jenny suggested that because she would not be able to show the completed effort in person, she e-mail "before and after" photos of each of these objectives to her counselor. Another client, Sharon, developed a similar goal and applied Jenny's idea to take and send photographs via text message. Sharon found that "having to e-mail pictures really helped me make sure I did it. And *really* did it." Jenny also expressed increased motivation and feelings of accountability as a result of having to e-mail her photos. If you are not working with a professional, agree to send photos to a family member or friend—anyone to whom you can be accountable.

Both women also reported that looking at the photos produced a sense of accomplishment. In addition, "before" photos can serve as cautionary reminders of what not to go back to, and "after" photos help to remind you how the organized space should look. Keep printouts of such photos on the corresponding space: the closet door, desk, or shelves. These can serve not only as visual aids in maintaining the system you worked so hard to create, but also as a way to provide you with a sense of achievement every time you walk by and see the changes you made.

Before and After Photos

Sharon's "before" desk photograph.

Sharon's "after" desk photograph.

Sharon's "before" shelves photograph.

Sharon's "after" shelves photograph.

Pick a Spot

Do you come home from work thirsty and your keys end up in the refrigerator? Have you ever found your wallet soaking wet at the bottom of the washing machine? Could you have a party made up entirely of people who have found your cell phone at one time or another? One of the most frustrating things about living with ADHD can be the tendency to lose or misplace those everyday items like keys, cell phones, and wallets. For items such as these, the best rule you can create for yourself is to have a specific place to put them each and every day. You probably don't often lose your toothbrush. This is because since you were a young child you have made a habit of keeping it in a toothbrush holder right next to the sink. You can develop similar habits for the other small daily-use items through routine and strategic placement.

Timing is also critical. The closer to the door you can empty your pockets, the better, because the more time you spend in the home or office getting distracted by other things, the less likely these items are to make it to their spot.

Here is a list of good spots for some of those everyday items:

1. For keys, hang up a row of key hooks right under the light switch located just inside the front door so that as your hand reaches for the switch, you only have to move inches to drop your keys into place. And just in case you do lose your keys, keep an extra set in a safe yet memorable place.
2. Just under this area, place a small table. On top of the table put a basket or tray for your wallet, watch, or other

frequently used items. Keep a similar container on your bed-room dresser, kitchen counter, or desk. Then make a rule that these items are only allowed in one of these containers.

3. The only time your cell phone should be allowed outside of the tray or basket is when you are using it or charging it. For charging, purchase an inexpensive charging station so that you always use the same outlet and place the cell phone there every evening.

In Sight, in Mind

Do you stick important papers all over your home or office and forget about their very existence? Or maybe you sometimes make the effort to file papers away but either forget that you did or where you put them within your files? Have you often found moldy food in the vegetable drawer of your refrigerator? Have you splurged on an outfit, stuck it in the back of your closet, and then bought another exactly like it months later? Because of distractibility and forgetful-ness, most adults with ADHD struggle with keeping track of any-thing that doesn't jump out at them visually. You don't have to be a victim to this "out of sight, out of mind" tendency. Instead, keep things in sight and in mind.

Unfortunately, your house isn't made of Plexiglas. Still, there are many things you can do to increase the visibility of your items:

1. Avoid closed filing cabinets. Instead, use a vertical filing system placed on an open bookcase. Every office supply

store carries stackable hard plastic open shelves that you can label for important papers and small items.

2. Use transparent plastic containers (the kind for storing food will do) for office supplies and other small items.

3. Post appointments, schedules, to-do lists, and the like in prominent areas at home or the office. Keep these papers off tables or desks where they will get covered. Instead, hang them on walls or mirrors (the bathroom mirror is a great spot).

4. Keep notepads and sticky notes in useful locations, such as in the car or beside your bed, to use for writing down thoughts and ideas as they pop into your head. Just make sure the notes then get rewritten in your planner or agenda so that they do not get lost or forgotten.

5. Color code. People with ADHD often are visually oriented. When you can associate a particular item with a color, it becomes more memorable. For filing, use colorful folders and tie the first letter of the subject matter to the first letter in a color. For example, "taxes" could be tangerine, "medical" could be maroon.

6. Put medication in a bright, obnoxious-looking cookie jar placed right next to the coffee maker. Then place a sign on the coffee maker that states, "Don't forget your cookies!" Good for a morning laugh, too.

7. Put shortcuts to important computer files directly on your desktop screen with names such as "Finances_CHECK

DAILY," make a daily to-do list document your screen saver, or start your computer with a silly but helpful password such as "dontforgetbills2012."

CAN YOU RELATE TO THIS?

The following describes the case of a young mother of four, Cindy. Cindy was diagnosed with ADHD as an adult and struggled with depression as a result of her ADHD symptoms. Her marriage was suffering, she could not hold down a job, and she was rarely engaging with her four sons. Cindy sought help for her ADHD with the idea that she somehow wanted to organize her home, spend more time with her kids, and make some money for the family so as to reduce the tension between her husband and herself.

Cindy spoke rapidly and intensely in her first session (some adults with ADHD manifest their hyperactivity verbally rather than physically). She felt she was sliding deeper and deeper into depression as a result of her inability to cope with her ADHD symptoms. She once had a fast-paced, high-profile career in which she used her ADHD tendencies to her advantage. Her job involved building social networks and being able to quickly jump from one task to the next. Needless to say, she excelled at it. But with the decision to quit and with the birth of each child, she began losing her sense of self and having trouble with the routine and isolating tasks of a stay-at-home mom. "I feel like such a loser that I can't even manage to do the laundry and get it folded in the same day," Cindy whispered, "and I have bought the kids so many clothes and toys that have barely been used. Some things even have the tags still on them. And they are just sitting there, making our house a mess."

While she processed her depression and set a goal to stabilize her emotional state, Cindy decided to set an additional goal to "create and follow through with a schedule of organizing the children's clutter." To begin work on this goal, Cindy's first objective was to think in terms of improving the organization of her space, not perfecting it. She wrote three notes with the phrase "Progress Not Perfection" and taped them to her children's playroom, her bedroom closet, and the children's closet. Then Cindy and her counselor decided on the order in which she would tackle the spaces. Cindy decided her own closet would be the easiest and therefore put it first, next the children's closet, and finally the playroom. She found organizing inherently boring and completely unmotivating. Instead, she valued being able to contribute monetarily to her family, spend time with her kids, and make her husband proud. Therefore, Cindy and her counselor created an incentive for her to do all three while ultimately meeting her organization goal: Cindy would organize the items with her children's help, then locate consignment sales in the area and sell her items there.

Cindy used the pile system mentioned previously to separate her items. She set a kitchen timer for 30 minutes each day, worked with her older boys to decide where to put things, then laid out the items on blankets in her bedroom. Her 6-year-old son, Danny, who was learning to tell time, reveled in his job of giving each item a 1-minute time limit for a pile decision. Once mom reached her time limit, he would make a loud "beeeeeep!" sound, imitating a game-show buzzer. Cindy chuckled in session as she remembered, and a tear came to her eye as she said, "I haven't had that much fun with my children in months." Once they were done each day, Cindy and the kids put the items in large trash bags, labeled them, and moved them into the basement.

In the meantime, Cindy researched and committed to several consignment sales in the area, each about 1 month apart. She also noted the dates by which she had to have her items to each site. Cindy specifically decided to work with 1-day events rather than consignment stores so that she would have firm due dates. "It helps me with my accountability," she affirmed. "I have people counting on me, and my things are needed on a particular day. It helps keep me on track and makes me feel like part of a team again." As Cindy's confidence began to grow and she started to see the literal payoff from all of her hard work, her depression began to lift. Even her husband became more attentive—not only was his wife contributing financially to the family once again, but more important, he also saw a shift in her mood and responsiveness with their children, to which he was very attracted.

Help Yourself! Challenge Your Fears

Think of an area in your home or office that you would like to organize. Write that area here: _____

Write down your fears about organization. On the next line, write a "challenge thought":

Fear 1: _____

Challenge Thought: _____

Fear 2: _____

Challenge Thought: _____

Fear 3: _____

Challenge Thought: _____

Fear 4: _____

Challenge Thought: _____

Fear 5: _____

Challenge Thought: _____

Now complete the phrase: "It's _____, NOT _____"
and repeat it out loud to yourself five times.

Next, decide what is motivating you to organize this particular space.
Write it here:

_____

_____

_____

_____

Decide how you are going to break down your space into smaller segments in order to keep you from becoming overwhelmed. List those
areas here beginning with the easiest:

_____

_____

_____

_____

On your own or with the help of a friend or professional, create a specific
plan for organizing your space. If it is a closet, perhaps you would like to

(*continues*)

Help Yourself! Challenge Your Fears (*Continued*)

separate types of clothing (blouses, pants, skirts, etc.) and create an area
for shoes. For a desk, perhaps you need an inbox and outbox, and a place
to store office supplies. Describe your vision for your space below:

_____

_____

_____

_____

Draw a picture of what you would like the space to look like when you
have completed it:

Now decide which rules you are going to apply when organizing this space
(e.g., "keep, throw or donate," photographs, pick a spot, using a timer).
Be creative—feel free to make up your own rules in addition to the ones
in this chapter. Write them here as they relate to this particular space:

Rule: _____ Application: _____

Rule: _____ Application: _____

Rule: _____ Application: _____

Help Yourself! Challenge Your Fears *(Continued)*

Rule: _____ Application: _____

Rule: _____ Application: _____

Rule: _____ Application: _____

Congratulations! You are on your way toward creating a functional and organized space! As you begin to follow through with your plan, remember to work for small periods of time so as not to become overwhelmed or distracted. And don't forget to take a photo of your final product to showcase as evidence that yes, you can be organized!

 AFTER GETTING ORGANIZED

Often, the hardest part of organizing for an adult with ADHD isn't the creation of an organizational system but rather the maintenance of it, or *keeping* it organized. Several strategies can help you maintain a streamlined space and keep clutter from coming back.

Most important, to help you keep perspective, tell yourself up front that there will be times when your space won't be as organized as others are, and that is okay. Life happens. You should expect that while Aunt Marge and Uncle Herb are visiting, you will fall out of your routine a bit and things might get a little messy. Or a couple of busy days at the office may make it literally impossible to do much beyond feeding the kids and putting them to bed before nearly passing out yourself. The mail will come every day, groceries will need to be bought and put away, and you will continue to receive invoices at work. However, you will recover, and now you have the skills to do so. Organizing isn't a one-time task. Even with proper maintenance, you may need to do a "spring cleaning" every year (or month).

Some of the ideas set forth in regard to *during* organization can also apply to *after* getting organized. For example:

- Look at *before* and *after* photographs to help you stay motivated and to remember what a space should look like.
- Put everyday items in their spot immediately after each time they are used.

Here are some other ideas to help you to stay organized:

1. Do a quick clean up at the end of each day. Take 10 to 15 minutes to do a sweep of your home or office and pick up and put items away that got overlooked or misplaced during the day.
2. For more time-consuming organizational tasks such as sorting mail and bills, filing papers, or online banking, schedule a set day and time each week to complete the task. Make it a rule. For example, "Every Thursday night before dinner I do laundry."
3. For each new item you bring into your home, get rid of one item. This will help you to avoid creating more clutter and cause you to stop and think about whether you

really need something new over something else you already own.

4. Follow the "Handle It Once" rule for sorting mail or papers. When it is time to do your weekly sorting, do not create more piles to go through later. Junk mail gets immediately tossed in the trash or recycling bin. Bills get paid right then and there, and important papers get filed away into your superbly organized, color-coded filing system.

5. Keep small containers in several rooms of your house or one in your office that you can use to collect items that are out of place. Then (immediately) take a second walk around, putting the items back where they belong.

6. For e-organization on your computer or portable electronic device use programs such as Evernote or The Personal Brain, which allow you to save ideas through pictures, webpages, or handwritten notes and then organize and find them easily.

Another helpful ongoing conversation to have with yourself is about the way in which you think about clutter. You may have an aversion to getting rid of things for fear that you might someday need them, but make sure to give yourself a reality check. *Clutter* includes those items in your home or office that serve no practical purpose and rarely, if ever, get used. *Practical* can mean it serves a function such as a can opener might, or it somehow enhances your mental and emotional well-being, like that framed photo of you and your dog camping at the lake. However, if an item doesn't fall into one of these categories, you probably don't need it. Use this worksheet to decide what to keep and what to toss in an effort to maintain organization in your space:

Organization Worksheet			
Item	Purpose	Last time it was used	Keep or throw
_____	_____	_____	_____
_____	_____	_____	_____
_____	_____	_____	_____
_____	_____	_____	_____

SUMMARY

Here are the important points you will want to take away from this chapter. Use the following checklist to note the areas you have thoroughly studied. Leave the box empty if it is an area you would like to come back to and review further.

☐ I understand how ADHD impacts my difficulty with organization.

☐ I have discovered the reasons I want to get organized.

☐ I have created a list of the areas I would like to organize and numbered the list from most important to least important.

☐ Using the suggestions, I have decided how I will organize my space prior to diving in.

☐ I have learned to tackle one space at a time.

☐ I have decided what specific tips I will use while organizing my space.

☐ I have learned several ways to maintain the organization of my space.

CHAPTER SIX

PRACTICING EFFECTIVE LEARNING AND STUDY SKILLS

Give me six hours to chop down a tree, and I will spend the first four sharpening the axe.

—Abraham Lincoln

 There is absolutely no evidence that adults with ADHD are not as smart as other adults. If you have been accused of being stupid or lazy, we hope you have ignored that, because chances are you are just as bright as, and perhaps work even harder than, your friends, classmates, or colleagues. However, the core symptoms of ADHD (impulsivity, inattention, and hyperactivity) can wreak havoc on your best-laid plans to study or write a report or take a test. In this chapter, we're going to get down to the nuts and bolts of studying, memorizing, paying attention, taking notes, reading without your mind wandering, and writing a paper. Because these are primarily strategies that you need in an educational setting, much of this chapter is geared toward college students; however, the basic skills can easily be applied to work settings also. Start by taking the quiz and finding out whether you see yourself in this chapter.

QUIZ YOURSELF—DOES THIS SOUND LIKE YOU?

1. Are the notes you take in class or meetings not very helpful to you later?
2. Do you have a hard time figuring out what to include in your notes?
3. Do you read something and then quickly forget it?
4. Can you read a chapter several times without it really sinking in?
5. Do you study for tests or prepare for presentations but then go blank when it's time to recall the information?
6. Do you feel you spend far more time than others studying or preparing or none at all because you have given up?

WHAT THE EXPERTS SAY

When college students with ADHD are asked to describe their learning and test-taking strategies and then are compared with college students without ADHD, we find that the students with ADHD self-report more difficulties in eight of 10 areas. Many of these areas can be applied to the world of work as well. Let's go through these one by one.

1. *Concentration:* Not surprisingly, students with ADHD have a harder time concentrating. They have reported that their mind wanders when studying; they don't listen carefully in

class; they tend to think about other things during lectures; and once they lose focus, they have a hard time getting it back.

2. *Time management:* Students with ADHD are more likely to procrastinate and put off studying until the last minute, so that they wind up "cramming" to prepare for an exam. They are not as likely to set up a study schedule, or if they do, they aren't as likely to stick to the schedule.

3. *Integrating information:* Students with ADHD are not as likely to use techniques to help them integrate and understand the things they are studying. Students without ADHD are more likely to try and relate material to their own life, fit it together logically, or put it into their own words to make it more understandable.

4. *Self-testing:* Students with ADHD are less likely to use strategies such as reviewing their notes after class or before tests or making up possible test questions to help them learn material.

5. *Selecting main ideas:* Students with ADHD have a difficult time figuring out the important information in a lecture or in something they are reading. They tend to get lost in the details and wind up missing the big picture or main point.

6. *Test strategies:* Students with ADHD are not very good at preparing for tests; they report not being good at studying in general, don't know how to change their study habits according to the type of course or exam, and take too long to study. They also do poorly on tests, even when they know the information, because they misunderstand the directions or fail to review their answers.

7. *Motivation:* Students with ADHD find it hard to keep going when they find a subject dull or uninteresting. They aren't as likely to self-motivate themselves by setting goals, and they are more likely to give up easily when work is hard.

8. *Anxiety:* Students with ADHD are more likely to report that both studying and taking exams were hampered because they felt anxious about doing poorly.

The positive news is that there are two areas in which adult students with ADHD tend to do just as well in as students without ADHD.

1. *Study aids:* Students with ADHD tend to use websites and learning centers just as frequently as students without ADHD. They ask partners to study with them, go to review sessions, and talk with instructors. Students with ADHD generally know and understand what they need to do; they just don't always implement the detailed strategies or follow through on things that involve motivation and concentration.

2. *Attitudes:* Students with ADHD have the same level of interest in school as their peers and find college worthwhile. Although their motivation and follow-through may be poor, their attitude toward education in general is very positive.

It's fairly common to find that college students with ADHD have a lower grade-point average and are more likely to be on academic probation than those without ADHD. Adults with ADHD are also more likely to be laid off, impulsively quit jobs, or be reprimanded at work (more on this in Chapter 7). Why is this? It seems to come down to the specific symptoms of ADHD that keep people from reaching their potential. For example, Tony, a college sophomore with ADHD, knew how to study; he was bright and had pretty good academic skills. However, when Tony left his dorm and headed for the library to study, he would often encounter an "obstacle." Some days he would run into a friend who would convince him to go to the gym, some days he would realize he had forgotten the right folder and head back to his dorm, and some days he would make it all the way to the library but be "waylaid" by the coffee shop just inside the front door and wind up having a latte and chatting with friends. Tony knew *what* he needed to do; he just couldn't quite get to the point where he actually *did* it.

As discussed in earlier chapters, a basic difficulty for those with ADHD is *self-regulation*. Self-regulation is one of the core determinants of behavior and includes several different skills that, when combined, allow you to control and change your behaviors. These behaviors are critical in affecting future actions so that you can attain your goals. When students or workers are unable to self-regulate, they are affected in many ways, such as when taking notes, listening in lectures or meetings, studying for tests, writing papers or reports, or taking exams. Researchers have found that in a learning environment, adults with ADHD are not as adept at summarizing and outlining. You may tend to give up and need looming deadlines to get started. You may also take longer to accomplish the same task as someone without ADHD because you have trouble remembering and applying what you have just read. It's not so much that you can't do these tasks, but rather that you have difficulty regulating these tasks. So we're going to spend some time in this chapter going over some of the basic skills needed in these areas.

But first, let's start with one last research study to give you some positive motivation. This study was done by Patricia Kaminski and her colleagues at the University of North Texas.[1] Rather than asking students with ADHD about their problems, the researchers asked them what helped them to succeed. See if the following top five strategies surprise you:

1. The number one key to success was working longer and harder than other students.
2. The number two response was using some type of social support (getting help from parents, friends, roommates, and professors). Many colleges and universities have specific offices or centers designed to help students who have learning difficulties, ADHD, or specific disabilities.
3. Being organized, managing their time, and using good study skills were important strategies mentioned.
4. Exercise helped students have the energy to get things done.
5. Keeping a positive mental attitude was important.

[1]Kaminski, P. L., Turnock, P. M., Rosén, L. A., & Laster, S. A. (2006). Predictors of academic success among college students with attention disorders. *Journal of College Counseling, 9,* 60–71.

☞ CAN YOU RELATE TO THIS?

The following vignette describes a typical college student with ADHD. See if any of this sounds familiar to you.

Robert was a sophomore in college, majoring in criminal justice. He hoped to go into law enforcement after graduation and perhaps work for the FBI one day. He thought he would begin the process by becoming a police officer in his home town, where both his father and grandfather had been on the police force. Robert sought treatment for his ADHD after being put on academic probation. He reported that he had had difficulty in high school and had never been a very good student. He was outgoing and popular, and spent more time in social activities than on his schoolwork. He had several friends and girlfriends who would help him out, and he managed to get average grades. Robert stated that his teachers always seemed to like him; he went for help frequently, did extra credit work when he could, and sometimes "got a grade I probably didn't deserve" because of his positive attitude. Robert was surprised he had actually been accepted to a large state university and felt very fortunate to be there. He was very motivated regarding his academic performance and wanted very badly to do well, but he struggled to keep up with his classes. Robert suspected that he had ADHD; he had been told by his advisor that he exhibited many of the symptoms, but he had never been formally diagnosed.

Robert reported that he was "barely scraping by" in college. It was no longer possible to charm his teachers into giving him grades he probably didn't deserve. He reported that despite his best intentions, he just couldn't seem to keep up. He felt that he had never really learned how to study or take notes or write papers. Robert reported that he would often plan to go to the library for an entire evening to catch up on his work. He would arrive, pick out a seat, and spend half an hour sharpening his pencils, organizing his notebooks, and "settling in." He would go get a cup of coffee and drink it before returning to his seat. Then he would check his cell phone and answer a few text messages. He wasn't sure what happened next, but somehow a couple of hours would go by and he wouldn't have accomplished anything. When he finally settled in to read something, he would read it over and over without remembering much about it. Robert reported that it took him about 4 hours at the library to do 20 minutes of work. As a result, he was constantly behind.

When his counselor asked about upcoming assignments, Robert reported that he had a major paper due about the role of race and culture on perceptions of competence for a psychology class. He was already overwhelmed. He had actually read 20 different sources and had about 25 pages of notes, but he was struggling with how to take all the notes and turn them into a paper. When asked if he had created an outline, he sheepishly admitted that he didn't really know how to do that. During a later session, Robert brought his notes. He had cut and pasted lots of good research, statistics, and background information from a wide variety of online sources and had an impressive amount of material. But he was stumped about how to integrate all this into a paper.

After extensive discussion between Robert and his counselor, it was clear that his strong points were his motivation, attitude, and interest in his future career. He showed a relative strength in math and had done well in his algebra class. However, Robert had never developed good study skills, particularly with regard to reading, taking notes, and writing papers. The good news was that the foundational strategies he was missing could be fairly easily learned. Robert enrolled in a class called Academic Success offered at his university. This class helped him with strategies such as organization, time management, and using a planner. In addition, he worked for 8 weeks with an ADHD coach who did in-depth work on his specific areas of need. They practiced efficient note taking, and she helped him develop a strategy for writing his term paper. Consistent with his past performance, Robert was a pleasure to work with. He remarked several times, "I can't believe I never knew this!" or "This is so easy when you know what you're doing!"

We see quite a few "Roberts" in our work. These are students who have received help in getting schoolwork done over the years but have never really learned the skills to complete things on their own efficiently. Sometimes the complaint that it takes them three times longer than their friends to accomplish things is primarily because of distractibility and lack of concentration. Other times it's because they don't have the basic know-how to get the task done. One such student told a story about the time she and a big group of friends had gone camping and set up all their tents, using a frying pan to knock in the stakes. Had they thought to bring a hammer, they could have done it much quicker. Sometimes the answer to your difficulties is as easy as replacing your frying pan with a hammer!

GETTING BACK ON TRACK: STUDY STRATEGIES

Adults with ADHD frequently state how surprised they are at the differences between studying for college-level courses and those they had in high school. Many students with ADHD report that they were able to make *A*s and *B*s in high school, often without trying too hard. This may have been the case for you. However, in high school you benefited from regular homework, frequent worksheets or quizzes, and a grade that depended on many samples of your work. You also may have relied on parents in high school to help you stay organized, focused, and on schedule. Then, in college, these strategies just weren't working. You weren't used to writing long papers, or having to memorize a semester's worth of facts for a final exam, or having to explain and integrate conceptual information. Sometimes it isn't school at all that brings out these weaknesses but rather a particular job that requires new skills. Many adults with ADHD seek help in adapting their study habits to the college, graduate school, or work setting. There are several steps involved in making the transition to higher level studying, so let's start at the beginning.

Get Off to a Good Start

- Before class starts, find out what the book is and buy it. If the syllabus is online, read it before class starts.
- Go to every lecture. Sit in the front. Take notes. Ask questions. Engage. Turn off your cell phone.
- Write assignments for the semester in your planner. Make a study schedule.

- Do the homework or readings. Be prepared for class. Read your syllabus weekly.
- Take care of yourself. Eat, sleep, and exercise to stay healthy.
- You can't be studying if you're partying. Make time every week to study.
- Go talk to the instructor or teaching assistant. Think of questions you can ask.
- Don't wait until the last minute to study or do assignments and projects.

A recent study conducted at Rio Salado, a small Arizona community college, showed that one behavior was the best predictor of students doing well in their college classes.[2] What would you guess it was? IQ? High school grades? Easiness of the subject matter? Actually, it was none of the above. The single best predictor of doing well in college classes was whether the student went online the week before class and opened the syllabus. Surprised? It really does make sense. The type of student who does that is usually the same type of student who prepares in advance, in general. The same is true for working adults. That may not yet be you, but it's a good practice to get into. Next, we're going to cover some basic suggestions for how, when, and where to study. We'll follow those up with some more specific study skills.

---

[2]Kolowich, S. (2009, October 30). The new diagnostics. *Inside Higher Ed*. Available at http://www.insidehighered.com/news/2009/10/30/predict

General Suggestions for Studying

1. Spending long hours studying is not necessarily productive. In fact, if you have ADHD, it's likely to be counterproductive. You're much better off if you select several small chunks of time; 20- to 50-minute time periods followed by a brief break (5–10 minutes) is a more effective way to study.

2. Picking a good place to study is crucial. You know where you'll be distracted. Don't go there! Turn off the TV. Some people can study with an iPod or music playing in the background, and this can serve to drown out other noise. Figure this out for yourself. If the music is helpful, use it.

3. Discover your ideal time to study. This may be first thing in the morning or late at night. Figure out your peak times and use them.

4. Start with the hard stuff. That way, when you are getting tired or bored or want to give up, you can reward yourself by switching to something relatively easier.

5. Make sure that you understand the assignment before you start, so that you can plan your time efficiently. Don't waste time by doing work you don't really need to be doing.

6. Sit in a comfortable chair at a table. Get out of the habit of studying in bed. Don't confuse your body. Train it that bed means *sleep* and chair/table means *read*. (This will also help if you have trouble sleeping.)

7. Get in the habit of doing something every day. If you do even a half hour of good work each day, at the end of the week you will have done 3 hours of studying. It's really

easy to procrastinate and have nothing accomplished at the end of the week.

8. Reward yourself. Try small rewards after 30 minutes of studying (a snack?) and bigger rewards after a week of meeting goals (go to the mall?). For more on rewards, go back and review Part I on goal setting.

9. Work with others when appropriate. Not only can this be more enjoyable, but you can also gain motivation from them and they can help keep you on track. But pick your study partners carefully; try to select those with good study habits and see if you can learn some of their strategies.

10. Study early and often. Research has shown that cramming is an ineffective way to study.

Note Taking

There are two typical sources for studying: one is your notes from class (or meetings if you are at work), and the other is reading material (books, articles). It's hard to study notes that are poorly written. So the next section focuses on note-taking skills. One very useful and popular method of note taking is called the *Cornell method*. This system was devised in the 1950s by Walter Pauk, an education professor at Cornell University. Next, we

Dragon Dictation is a mobile application that allows users to verbally dictate notes to a scratch-pad, then edit via voice or keyboard icon. It is a great option if you have trouble writing fast enough to cover everything in a lecture or meeting.

describe the basic approach, but we have modified it somewhat to make it meet the needs of students with ADHD.

1. *Get organized:* Make sure you have a good system for keeping your notes. You might prefer one notebook for every subject or loose-leaf paper inside a three-ring binder. Whatever works for you is fine, but it is important that you have a consistent system so that you can always have your notes together and find them when you need them. Now, on each page of your paper, draw a vertical line. You should have twice as much space on one side as on the other (see the following sample).

2. *During class or meetings:* Take your notes on the larger section. Don't write full sentences. Key words and phrases are better. Try to learn some symbols or abbreviations.

3. *Review:* Do this directly after your class or meeting if possible. If not, do it soon, while your short-term memory is still working. Fill in any gaps in your notes. Underline or jot down anything you might need to ask the instructor or a colleague to clarify. On the right-hand side of the paper, write study questions that are based on your notes.

4. *Study:* When you're ready to study, cover the notes side of your paper. Read your questions and answer them. Do this out loud if possible. It helps the transfer to long-term memory.

5. *Reflect:* Try to make the material meaningful. Think to yourself: What's the significance of these facts? What principle are they based on? How can I apply them? How do

Sample Notes and Review Questions	
Notes	**Questions**
Popular system = Cornell method	*What's the name of a popular note-taking system?*
Organize—draw line	
Class—use shorthand	*How many minutes should you spend reviewing prior notes each week?*
Review—fill in, write questions	
Short-term memory (ask teacher	
how long short-term memory lasts)	
Study—cover one side	
Weekly = 10 minutes old notes	

they fit in with what I already know? What's beyond them? Can I relate them to my own life? This also helps make the transition to long-term memory.

6. *Every week:* Spend at least 10 minutes reviewing all your previous notes.

General Suggestions for Reading

Another common complaint from adults with ADHD is that they read an entire chapter or article, only to realize they have no clue what they just read. Much of this has to do with the distractibility and inability to focus that are inherent in ADHD. So let's start this section again with some general suggestions on reading and focusing, and then go into some more specific strategies.

1. Rather than remembering facts, focus on making the material meaningful. How does it fit with what you already know?

How can you apply it? What questions does it create for you? What broad category would you fit it into?

2. Reading a chapter one time actively (making notes, summarizing, creating questions, analyzing) will benefit you much more than reading it many times passively.

3. One method of active reading is to read a paragraph, close your book, and recite out loud everything you remember in your own words. We promise you, if you do this, it's impossible to read a whole chapter and ever again say, "I have no clue what I just read."

4. Some things just have to be memorized. When you come to those, make a list, and then refer to the following section on memory skills for tips on how to remember the list.

5. Graphic organizers can help those who process information or learn visually by mapping ideas as pictures. For example, remembering the colors of a rainbow becomes much easier after drawing a rainbow, rather than simply listing the colors in order. This idea can be applied in creative ways with almost any type of reading or study material.

HELP YOURSELF! IMPROVE YOUR CONCENTRATION

Are you able to read a mystery novel for hours at a time, but after sitting down to read 10 pages of your anthropology homework or work report, you realize you don't remember a single word? It's clear you have the ability to focus; you just need to train your mind to focus on things that are not inherently interesting or immediately rewarding to you. The trick to this is a combination of (a) preparation for concentration, (b) arranging your external environment, and (c) self-regulating your thoughts. These are skills that take practice, just like anything else. Your mind is used to wandering, and you let it do that. But you can train yourself to concentrate. It takes practice, just like any other skill.

You can begin by practicing immediate awareness. You need to train yourself to be alert each time your mind starts to wander. Start by using a pencil and making a small mark at the end of each sentence if you have not fully concentrated on that sentence. Don't let yourself progress to the next sentence unless you have concentrated on the one at hand.

You also need to practice ignoring. Let's say you're reading and you hear your phone signal that you have a text message. Ignore it (you should have turned the phone off, right? But perhaps you didn't). Just keep reading. Next, someone walks by your seat in the library and you're tempted to look up and see who it is. Resist the urge to look up. By practicing this, you can begin to train your mind to ignore distractions. Don't forget to immediately reward yourself when you resist distraction. Maybe you should keep a favorite (healthy) snack nearby, and take a bite every time you successfully ignore something tempting.

There are some other tricks that will help you concentrate on what you are reading. When your mind begins to wander, stop and immediately focus on the last sentence you remember. Train your mind to focus. Read the sentence out loud if you're in a private area or mouth the words if you're in public. Visualize the sentence in your mind and try to create an image of what it is conveying. Focus intently on that one sentence. If there's a word in the sentence that you don't understand, go ahead and look it up. Try writing down the one or two key terms in the sentence. This may seem like a really slow process, but it's much speedier than "waking up" after 10 minutes and realizing you comprehend nothing of what you have just read.

Don't try to read too much at one time. Vary the activity. If you have read and focused well for 15 minutes, stop and do something different. Do a worksheet. Update your planner. Create some sample test questions. Answer a few math problems. Then go back to reading. If you find yourself distracted by extraneous thoughts or ideas, keep a sheet of paper handy and write the thought or idea down. This can help you to let it go until later when you have time to deal with it. Also, don't set yourself up for failure. Plan to read when you are most alert. If you feel yourself drifting off, get up for a few minutes, wash your face, have a snack, or do a few brief exercises.

 TRY IT! UNDERSTAND AND APPLY WHAT YOU READ

This next section gives you some suggestions on how to really understand what you read. Before you begin to read, start with some careful preparation. If there's an introduction or outline, read through that so you can get your mind ready. This is similar to reading the menu and placing your order before you eat a meal in a restaurant. It helps to know what's coming; it sort of sets up your taste buds to appreciate the food. Just skim through the chapter and notice the headings. Try to think in advance about what you will read and how you might apply it. Is this a totally new area, or can you

K-W-L stands for "What I know," "What I want to know, and "What I learned." When reading about a new topic, try dividing your notes into these three sections. Fill out the K beforehand. Then after the first read-through, fill out sections W and L. This method will enhance your understanding and memorization of a new area of study.

relate it to something you already know? Actually write out a few questions you think you will need to answer or things you think you will need to memorize. Again, these steps are priming your mind to pay attention. Now, you're ready to read. Use the concentration suggestions in the previous section to keep you focused. Write down any answers to the questions you have posed. When you get to examples, go through each step. Mark anything you don't understand and look up words as needed.

When you are done, think back over what you've just read. Think about what you know now that you didn't know before. Jot down some possible exam questions, a brief outline, or some notecards. Do you have things you need to memorize? Make lists of those. Finally, go back regularly and briefly study your questions, outline, and note cards. You don't have to spend a great deal of time on this, just a brief review so that when it's time for the exam you won't need to cram.

Memory Skills

There are two types of memory that you need to do well in a higher learning environment and many employment settings. The first is remembering basic ideas that you will later use on essay type exams or reports. The second is verbatim memory of dates, formulas, names, specific facts, or foreign language words. In addition, just to get through the day, you need to remember appointments, class times, commitments, meetings, and due dates. A difficult time remembering things goes hand in hand with having ADHD. Here are some basic memory tips:

1. Before you try to memorize a concept, make sure you thoroughly understand the concept.
2. Make flashcards of things that you have to remember exactly, such as dates, foreign language vocabulary words, formulas, equations, and names.
3. Keep your flashcards handy and refer to them when you have short (10–15 minute) breaks.
4. Change the order of your flashcards occasionally to facilitate memory.
5. Try to create images in your mind of things you need to remember.
6. Make your own illustrations, such as maps, charts, and outlines. (Making them up creates memories, and referring back to them solidifies those memories.)
7. Draw pictures to illustrate things you need to remember.
8. Try to associate things you need to remember with things you already know. For example, you can remember that Mount Fujiyama is 12,365 feet high by associating it with a calendar (12 months, 365 days in a year).
9. Use the tried-and-true method of creating a sentence out of the first letters of the items you need to memorize. For

example, *a*luminum, *g*old, *o*xygen, *b*oron, *a*rsenic, *lith*-ium, *h*ydrogen, and *m*agnesium becomes *A g*ood *o*ld *b*oy *a*lways *l*oves *h*is *m*omma.

10. When studying for essay-type tests, try to explain an area or concept out loud to a friend or study partner in your own words.

Taking Tests

Now that you have studied and prepared for your test, you're ready to show off what you've learned. Make sure you get off to a good start. Arrive early for the test and select a seat in a location where you will not be distracted. It's usually better to sit in the front row, so you're not looking at the whole class. When you receive the test, review the whole thing and make sure you have all the necessary items including answer sheets, scantrons, and #2 pencils. Make sure you have read all the directions carefully. Many of our ADHD clients have reported that they rushed through the instructions or didn't read the questions carefully. Plan your test-taking strategy. Be sure you have brought something that keeps time, so you can monitor your progress. It's usually a good idea to answer some easy questions first to calm yourself down. Concentrate on working carefully but steadily. Keep your work neat; instructors can get cranky and view your work more negatively in general if they have a hard time deciphering it. Review your answers before you hand them in; don't second guess yourself, as your first instinct is usually correct, but do be sure you have read the question correctly. Don't worry about what other people are doing or when they are finishing. Think positively, and do your best.

For multiple choice tests, try to pick out two answers that you are fairly certain are incorrect. That only leaves you two choices, which increases your odds of choosing the correct answer to 50/50. For essay exams, try to write something for every question; otherwise, the instructor has no choice except to give you a zero. Try to jot down a brief outline of your answer with some key phrases or dates. Put them in order. It will help you to write an organized response, and then all you have to do is go back and fill in your outline. If you run out of time, you will likely get some credit for what you did. Write a first sentence for each paragraph that identifies the theme for that paragraph and make sure everything that follows fits in with that theme. If it doesn't, move it somewhere else.

Before turning in your exam, make sure you double check that all questions have been answered. After the exam, follow up. Even if you didn't do well, you can learn some things about yourself that can help you in the future. Ask yourself the following questions:

- What did I miss?
- Why did I miss it?
- Did I study the wrong thing?
- Did I study the right thing but didn't remember it effectively?
- Did I read the question wrong?
- Did I run out of time?
- Was I affected by anxiety?

Can you come up with some patterns that you can put to good use for your future studying? Identifying your own particular strengths and weaknesses is key to making improvements in your learning strategies.

Writing a Paper or Report

Many adults with ADHD report that they have a difficult time writing papers; it's hard for them to get started, hard to plan ahead and get things done in time, hard to organize their ideas, and hard to write things in a logical manner. The following suggestions will help you organize and write your research papers or work reports.

Step 1: Write a tentative title for your paper. Many times just selecting the title helps you to organize your thoughts. As an example, let's suppose you're writing a paper for your psychology class and you decide it will be about the effect of parental divorce on children.

Step 2: Write several bullet points describing your paper. These should be key topics that you think you want to cover. Any order is fine. For example, for the paper on divorce, your key topics might be as follows: Statistics about how many people get divorced, how is this bad for kids? Self-esteem? Parents who fight, does this matter? Depression in kids? Age of kids, does this matter? Gender of kids, does this matter? Does school work suffer? Are there any positive things about divorce? Is counseling helpful?

To reduce visual overload and avoid being overwhelmed by a large report with multiple topics, try writing each heading on a separate sheet of paper and addressing one idea at a time as if they were each a separate report.

Sample Outline for a Paper

The Effect of Parental Divorce on Children

1. Statistics
   A. Number of divorces
   B. Number of kids affected
2. Effects on kids
   A. Self-esteem
   B. Depression
   C. Poor school performance
   D. Other
3. Factors that make a difference
   A. Gender
   B. Age
   C. Parent Conflict
4. Counseling
5. Positive Aspects of Divorce
   References

Step 3: Outline what you are going to write about. Go back and organize the phrases above into an outline, using headings and subheadings. Group common thoughts together. Put them in a logical order. See the box above for an example.

Step 4: Do your research. You will likely do an online search of articles that have to do with parental divorce. If you can manage, the best way to take notes is to do it on your computer. This allows you to organize and move things around as you go. Organization of this material is the key to writing a successful paper.

Step 5: Organize your notes as you go. This may seem like a lot of work up front, but when you are through, the paper almost writes itself. When you review articles, *do not* organize your notes so that you wind up with one set of notes for each article you review. You will end up with a lot of information and a whole lot of work. Rather, go back to your outline and insert each separate idea. Let's say you are reading an article by Dr. Smith from 2009, and the first paragraph has some statistics about the frequency of divorce. Record the key information in your outline under the heading "Statistics/ Number of Divorces." Keep reading; you see some information about boys having a harder time when their fathers leave the home, so you record that under your outline heading "Factors That Make a Difference/Gender." Finally, you find some relevant information on group counseling for children of divorce, so you record that under the heading "Counseling." Before finishing, go ahead and write the entire Smith citation in a reference list. It's important to mention Smith (2009) every time you make a note, as this will keep you from plagiarizing. Now you're finished with the Smith article. Your second article is by Dr. Jones from 2008. Do the same thing, putting each piece of relevant information in its proper spot in the outline. If you read some information that you think is important but there's no heading in your outline that seems to fit, you have two choices: Either don't bother copying down that information because it's not relevant or add a new heading to your outline. Take a look at the sample on page 168 (note: references and information are fictional).

Step 6: Review your outline and notes. Do your notes seem to fit where you put things? Do you need to move them around? Sort notes within headings.

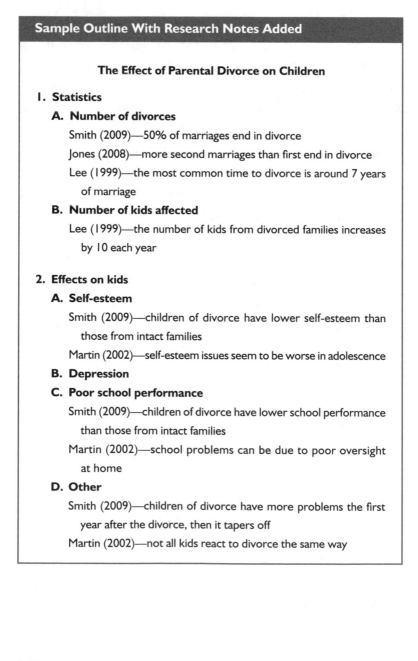

Sample Outline With Research Notes Added

The Effect of Parental Divorce on Children

1. **Statistics**
   A. **Number of divorces**
   Smith (2009)—50% of marriages end in divorce
   Jones (2008)—more second marriages than first end in divorce
   Lee (1999)—the most common time to divorce is around 7 years
   of marriage
   B. **Number of kids affected**
   Lee (1999)—the number of kids from divorced families increases
   by 10 each year

2. **Effects on kids**
   A. **Self-esteem**
   Smith (2009)—children of divorce have lower self-esteem than
   those from intact families
   Martin (2002)—self-esteem issues seem to be worse in adolescence
   B. **Depression**
   C. **Poor school performance**
   Smith (2009)—children of divorce have lower school performance
   than those from intact families
   Martin (2002)—school problems can be due to poor oversight
   at home
   D. **Other**
   Smith (2009)—children of divorce have more problems the first
   year after the divorce, then it tapers off
   Martin (2002)—not all kids react to divorce the same way

Sample Outline With Research Notes Added (Continued)

3. Factors that make a difference

A. Gender

Jones (2008)—girls seem to do better when they live with their mothers but this is not always true for boys

Martin (2002)—boys seem to need the discipline of a male figure

B. Age

Jones (2008)—it's a myth that older children do better than younger children

Smith (2009)—reviews 10 studies and concludes that age effects are inconsistent

C. Parent conflict

Smith (2009)—children of divorce do much worse when there is high parental conflict

Jones (2008)—parental conflict is the number one predictor of poor outcome

4. Counseling

Jones (2008)—group counseling can be very effective

Lee (1999)—cognitive–behavioral counseling has empirical support of effectiveness

Martin (2002)—many public schools provide group interventions for children of divorce

5. Positive aspects of divorce

Smith (2009)—children of divorce have reported being glad that the conflict has stopped

Martin (2002)—his study showed that children of divorce have a more realistic view of relationships

Jones (2008)—children of divorce reported that it made them stronger

(continues)

| **Sample Outline With Research Notes Added** *(Continued)* |

References

Jones, C. (2008). *Does conflict matter?* Washington, DC: American Psychological Association.

Lee, D. (1999). The effect of divorce on children and adolescents five years later. *Child Development, 12,* 33–45.

Martin, B. (2002). *Divorce: Research applications.* New York, NY: Guilford Press.

Smith, A. (2009). A longitudinal study of divorce. *Journal of Divorce, 15,* 209–221.

Step 7: Write your paper. This step will actually be very easy. You've got your paper outlined, it's in a logical order, and you have all the information you need. All you have to do is turn the phrases into sentences. For each heading in your outline, read through the notes you have put there and decide how many paragraphs you will need. Then write one lead thematic sentence for each paragraph and group the relevant notes under that paragraph. Now, take the remaining notes and write out the paragraphs.

Step 8: Review. Individuals with ADHD often report that the work they turn in is sloppy or has numerous errors. Therefore, don't forget this final step. Can you convince a friend or parent to review your paper when it's done? If not, go back and complete the following checklist:

____ I have a strong opening paragraph that lets the reader know what's coming.

_____ I have read the paper carefully for grammatical or spelling errors.

_____ I have started each paragraph with a thematic sentence.

_____ The sentences in each paragraph support the beginning thematic sentence.

_____ My paragraphs seem to be in a logical order.

_____ I have provided a summary at the end.

_____ All sources are cited properly to ensure that I am not plagiarizing.

GETTING BACK ON TRACK: HOW TO OVERCOME PERFORMANCE ANXIETY

Many of the clients we see who have ADHD also report being very anxious about school or work in general. Some of this is quite realistic. Common symptoms of ADHD can result in running out of time when taking tests, having a hard time getting started when trying to study, and losing focus when working. This history of not doing too well can become a self-fulfilling prophecy, and you can then become anxious just thinking about taking a test or starting a paper. Then the anxiety itself makes it more difficult to focus, and the whole thing snowballs. Scientists call this type of anxiety *evaluative stress* or *performance anxiety*. There seem to be two ways this anxiety comes out: One is cognitively and the other is physiologically. The first one we call worrying or thinking about your performance. The second one we'll call being emotional or "feeling" your worries internally. The physiological feelings include an increase in perspiration, respiration, heart rate, blood pressure, and muscle tension. Many people say that they feel like they have butterflies in their stomach. Both worry and feelings get in the way of studying, taking tests, or writing because they block your ability to think, to remember, and to produce new thoughts. It's pretty difficult to outline the events that led up to World War II if your mind is saying, "You're going to blow this test, you're going to fail this class, you're going to flunk out of school," or when you're trying to figure out if you're going to faint first or have a heart attack.

Basic Tips for Performance Anxiety

What can you do about this anxiety? One strategy is the *progressive relaxation* technique outlined in Chapter 8. This is something you can do regularly to reduce your overall level of anxiety. Once in the habit of doing this technique, you can easily do a shortened version in the library, before studying, and before exams. Here are some additional tips that will help you with anxiety:

1. Identify the thoughts that are causing your anxiety. Try to modify them.
2. Accept the anxiety. Accept that there will be questions whose answers you don't know. Accept your limits.
3. Work on your mental attitude. Realize that this one test or paper is just a part of your grade or life. Think about the things you do well and bear in mind that this test is not a measure of who you are.
4. Start your studying well in advance. Nothing creates more anxiety than waiting until the last minute and being panicked that it's too late.

5. Be better prepared. If you have studied well, you will be more confident in your abilities.

6. Learn effective test-taking strategies for different types of tests.

7. If time constraints and other students are distracting, seek accommodations. If you have a diagnosis of ADHD, you should qualify for extended time on tests or a nondistracting test environment.

8. Make sure you're prepared the night before a test with any materials you might need: a water bottle, your watch, a calculator, or other things you're allowed to bring with you.

9. Be sure to arrive at class on time, on even early, on the day of the exam.

10. Answer some easy questions first. Praise yourself when you answer a question.

Advanced Treatment for Test Anxiety

If these self-help strategies don't work for you, you might make an appointment with a psychologist and request a technique called *systematic desensitization*. Therapists use this strategy to work with individuals who have ADHD and severe test anxiety. Systematic desensitization has routinely been found to be one of the most successful behavioral treatments of anxiety and to be especially effective at decreasing the level of test anxiety and improving academic performance. Systematic desensitization starts with teaching you the progressive relaxation we mentioned above. The psychologist

Weekly Self-Evaluation for Studying

Check off the things you accomplished this week.

☐   I studied in a quiet place.

☐   I made a study schedule and kept to it.

☐   I completed all my homework assignments.

☐   I kept my folders, notebooks, and study area organized.

☐   I studied during my self-identified "peak period."

☐   I took notes in class and followed the note-taking suggestions.

☐   I used techniques to listen and focus better in class.

☐   I sat in the front of the class.

☐   I asked at least one question in class.

☐   If the teacher asked questions or asked for comments, I responded at least once.

☐   I reviewed and updated my notes fairly soon after class was over.

☐   I followed the suggestions in this book for reading.

☐   Each night I prepared for the day ahead (checked my calendar, got things I needed together).

Now, summarize your week:

The thing that worked best for me this week was _____

_____

The thing I wasn't too successful with was _____

_____

My goal for next week is _____

_____

will then work with you to create a personal anxiety hierarchy and spend several weeks combining relaxation with confronting and overcoming the elements on your own anxiety hierarchy. Over four to six sessions, this technique has proven to be effective for test anxiety.

Now that you've reviewed some general skills, try using the checklist on p. 174 each week to monitor your progress.

SUMMARY

To summarize, here are the important points you will want to take away from this chapter. Use the following checklist to note the areas you have thoroughly studied. Leave the box empty if it is an area you would like to come back to and review further.

☐ I understand the types of study and learning difficulties common in students with ADHD.

☐ I understand the areas in which students with ADHD seem to do as well as other students.

☐ I understand some keys to success reported by students with ADHD.

☐ I have started to prepare before class starts.

☐ I have learned new methods on how to take notes.

☐ I have learned how to read effectively.

☐ I have used new memory skills.

☐ I have learned skills for taking tests.

☐ I have learned how to write a paper.

☐ I have discovered ways to treat my test anxiety.

☐ I have done a weekly self-evaluation.

CHAPTER SEVEN

FINDING JOB SATISFACTION

Doing nothing is very hard to do . . . you never know when you're finished.

—Leslie Nielsen

 The world of work can be especially frustrating for adults with ADHD. Adults with ADHD tend to have held many different jobs and either were fired or quit after a short period of time, usually a year or less. Many report being late for work and not being able to get their work done. If you have ADHD, it is important that you choose a career that is compatible with your unique characteristics. This chapter will help you to choose a job that fits with your particular strengths and weaknesses. If you have already chosen a career path and feel now is not a time you can make a change, don't worry. We also provide some specific coping skills to help you succeed at your job, including suggestions for dealing with distractibility and lack of focus during the day. Finally, we give you information about workplace accommodations to which you might be entitled. Start by taking the quiz and finding out whether you see yourself in this chapter.

QUIZ YOURSELF—DOES THIS SOUND LIKE YOU?

1. Do you often fall behind or easily lose track of what you are supposed to be doing at work?
2. Does it take you longer than your coworkers to get the same thing done?
3. Is it difficult to get along well with your supervisor?
4. Are you unhappy in your current field but unsure of what job you would like better?
5. Do you often have a difficult time prioritizing your job duties?
6. Do you find it hard to concentrate on your work?
7. Is it hard to pay attention consistently in meetings or during presentations?
8. Are you often late for work or meetings?

WHAT THE EXPERTS SAY

Research has shown that in late adolescence, there seems to be no difference between the work performance of those with ADHD and those without ADHD. It is speculated that many jobs at this stage involve unskilled or semiskilled labor and that true differences may not be evident at this stage. However, by the time young adults graduate from college and take on more complex jobs, difficulties with ADHD emerge quite clearly. There are an estimated 8 million American adults with ADHD, and many of them find that working can be very challenging. One national survey showed that only half of adults with ADHD are able to hold down a full-time job, compared with 72% of adults who do not have ADHD.[1] Even when adults with ADHD do have a job, they tend to earn less, are promoted less frequently, and are less likely to become senior managers or have similar positions of authority. Adults with ADHD report more conflict with their supervisor and are more likely to receive disciplinary actions and negative performance evaluations. They are more likely than those without the disorder to hold down only a part-time job and to be fired from the job that they do hold. They are also more likely to switch jobs voluntarily, both because of their dissatisfaction in their present position and their need for change and new challenges. As a result, those with ADHD generally report more career dissatisfaction, confusion, anxiety, and conflict regarding their employment.

Let's go back to the three major symptoms of ADHD. Each can have a direct impact on work. For example, in the area of *inattentiveness*, common difficulties include not paying attention, making careless mistakes, not listening to directions, failing to finish assignments, trouble organizing tasks, becoming discouraged or giving up when a task takes sustained mental effort, and being easily distracted once a task is initiated. Cluttered desks, misplaced paperwork, and forgotten assignments are common. These symptoms can also be manifested as difficulty getting to work on time and procrastination with assigned duties. The ability to keep track of multiple deadlines and projects will be affected if one lacks organizational skills.

---

[1]ADD and ADHD Help Center. (2011). *WebMD.com*. Available at http://www.webmd.com/add-adhd/guide/adhd-in-the-workplace

With regard to symptoms of *hyperactivity*, workers with ADHD will have difficulty sitting still and completing tasks. They may find sitting through meetings excruciating and as a result miss quite a bit of information as they squirm, fidget, or take periodic breaks.

Finally, with regard to symptoms of *impulsivity*, adults with ADHD have a tendency to interrupt and blurt out answers before others have finished. This may make it difficult for them to work effectively with their colleagues. They may take on new tasks or volunteer for an assignment quite enthusiastically but then have difficulty with follow-through. The task may go unfinished, leaving them with the reputation of being unreliable. Their impulsivity appears to also be related to a difficulty in controlling emotions, which can be expressed as temper outbursts or angry comments. Some adults with ADHD may have frequent run-ins with coworkers or have a blow-up with their boss that results in their getting fired.

Numerous research studies have determined that adult workers with ADHD are more likely to exhibit the difficulties previously mentioned. There is direct evidence that the quality of their work differs significantly from that of adults without ADHD. Employers describe adults with untreated ADHD as less adequate at fulfilling work demands, less punctual, less likely to work independently and to complete tasks, and more likely to have a poorer overall work record. When asked to rate their most common symptoms of those just discussed, a large sample of adults with ADHD rated the top areas of difficulty (in order) as being distracted, fidgeting, having difficulty sustaining attention, and forgetting. The specific job duties that created difficulty were (in order) finishing the job, managing daily responsibilities, budgeting time, and meeting deadlines.

The degree to which a worker has difficulty is directly related to the number of ADHD symptoms he or she has. Workers in their mid-20s to mid-50s who have many symptoms of ADHD feel

> The degree to which a worker has difficulty is directly related to the number of ADHD symptoms he or she has.

anxious about making career decisions, are not comfortable taking responsibility for their career choices, and are less satisfied with their career choice.

There has been some controversy regarding the diagnosis of ADHD in adults with high IQ or high overall ability. Some people believe that if you are really successful, you can't possibly have ADHD. However, there are many instances of adults who do very well in high school and college and manage to cope with many of their symptoms, yet still have difficulty in their career. For example, someone may complete all the coursework for a PhD degree yet be unable to finish a dissertation. Another adult might be able to complete law school coursework but lacks the ability to study for and pass the bar exam. Very successful adults may still have a diagnosis of ADHD and may cope with their symptoms in some but not all situations. Take a look at this example: An extremely bright man in his 50s named Henry, who had previously been very successful in his career, sought treatment for his ADHD when he found himself struggling at his new job. He was a visionary and had been in a job in which a large support staff had relied on him to develop "big picture ideas" that they would then implement.

After changing jobs, Henry was required to do his own follow-through and attend to many more details. This job was incompatible with his ADHD symptoms, and he was struggling with his new responsibilities. Clearly, he was quite bright and had high overall ability; however, he did in fact have a diagnosis of ADHD, and the symptoms associated with this were impeding him in his new career.

A related enigma has to do with the fact that ADHD symptoms may not seem to emerge until one reaches a certain level of success. For example, a worker may do quite well in one job with low stress and fairly circumscribed job duties. However, a promotion to a higher level might require managerial and organizational skills and added job duties, resulting in increased stress. At this level of functioning, the worker with ADHD might find that his or her limits of productivity have been met, and he or she may not be able to handle the increased responsibilities of the job.

A final area of difficulty for adult workers can be the emotional problems that often accompany ADHD. These can be symptoms of depression and anxiety or a tendency to be angry and perhaps aggressive. Sometimes these symptoms can be a reaction to years of frustration, poor performance in school, and constant negative feedback or criticism. At other times, a psychological condition may coexist at the same time as the ADHD. Research has shown that if an individual has a diagnosis of ADHD, there is a higher than normal chance that he or she will also have a diagnosis of an additional psychological disorder. Regardless of the cause of this additional disorder, the added stress of dealing with emotional symptoms will make work performance and interacting with coworkers and supervisors more complicated. Please be sure to read Chapter 8 if you think that additional psychological disorders might be affecting your job performance.

 ## CAN YOU RELATE TO THIS?

The following vignette describes a woman with ADHD who sought help for work-related difficulties. See if any of this sounds familiar to you.

Audra was 45 years old and had never been diagnosed with ADHD; however, she had struggled her entire life at both school and work. In her current job she was responsible for tracking and maintaining a large database for a university student loan program. She encountered numerous difficulties in this job, and one of her coworkers suggested that she be evaluated for ADHD. Audra underwent a full evaluation by a psychologist and was diagnosed with ADHD, predominantly inattentive type.

During the evaluation, Audra reported that she worked late almost every night and all day Saturdays to keep up with her assignments. She was constantly in fear of being fired, and every time her supervisor asked to talk to her, she was sure he was going to tell her she was finished. During one meeting, her supervisor told her that her nickname in the department was "the black hole" and that coworkers complained that when they gave her something it would disappear, never to be seen again. He also told her that he was reluctant to assign new tasks to her, as he was pretty sure she wouldn't be able to complete them. This frequent negative feedback created a great deal of anxiety and further hindered Audra's daily performance. Audra's duties involved a variety of different tasks, including calling students, setting up files, maintaining databases, responding to inquiries, and problem solving whenever student loans were not processed correctly (which was often). She was constantly interrupted by phone calls that had to be dealt with immediately. She was also interrupted by coworkers who needed help with tasks that involved her. Audra could not deal with these interruptions and never seemed to get back on track afterward. At the end of each day, she felt that she had accomplished very little on her list of assigned tasks.

Audra explained to her counselor that she tried to keep a to-do list each day, but by noon she was so hopelessly behind that she usually abandoned it and just worked on whatever seemed to be a current crisis. Her desk was usually littered with files and paperwork, and she admitted that she was horrible at organizing her work and finding things that she needed. When she received a phone call, it frequently took an inordinate amount of time just to locate the relevant paperwork that the caller needed. Audra was particularly anxious about her supervisor's requests for information, as he generally stood in her doorway and glowered while she looked for the information he needed. During the previous month he had told her that she was "on report" and that her "remediation plan" was to organize her work space and increase the number of new cases she processed each week. Audra was despondent about these requests and had no idea how to get better organized.

Audra also felt that her coworkers were fed up with her. Many of their job duties were dependent on getting information from her. She would promise to have the information by a certain time, but she rarely managed to meet that commitment. Audra couldn't remember who she had made promises to. She usually wrote the requests on a note pad or sticky note but frequently lost the note. One of her coworkers, Evangeline, took pity on her and tried to give her suggestions about logging in requests, using a timer, making specific places for her folders, and keeping a daily to-do list. But Evangeline's rapid-fire description of the myriad things that Audra could do to improve her efficiency overwhelmed Audra even more, and she quickly lost her motivation to follow Evangeline's time-saving strategies.

Audra was also depressed about her personal life. She lived with her elderly parents, who had numerous medical problems and required several trips each month to various doctors. She frequently had to schedule these trips during the workday, which only compounded her work difficulties. Audra worried that something serious would happen to her parents and that she would not be able to cope with it. Her symptoms of depression and anxiety, coupled with her stresses at work, made her a "nervous wreck." She described her job and her life as one huge mountain that just kept getting steeper and steeper, while she kept sliding further and further downhill.

With regard to her early history, Audra reported that she had been a below-average student, managing to scrape by with a mostly C average. Her mother had helped her extensively during middle and high school and put her on a strict homework and activity schedule. Audra had lived at home during college, attending the local community college. Again, she had received help from her mother, along with tutoring and special assistance from her instructors. She had worked in a variety of jobs since college and had admittedly been a mediocre employee. She reported that she was frequently reprimanded for arriving late, not getting her work done, and being disorganized. No one had ever mentioned ADHD to her until her current coworker, Evangeline, had suggested that she might want to be tested. Audra was actually quite relieved when she received her diagnosis and said it felt as though the pieces all just clicked together and made perfect sense. She had answered positively to all 10 questions in the employment screener (see the Quiz on p. 178) and felt relieved that there was a reason for her work difficulties other than "just being stupid."

The case of Audra illustrates many difficulties experienced by adult workers with ADHD. Although it is not as likely that someone receives a first diagnosis of ADHD so late in life, it certainly happens, particularly for individuals who may have had good coping skills or support systems early on but who encountered increasingly more demands in new or different jobs. Audra's difficulties were primarily in the area of inattention, which is more common in adults than symptoms of hyperactivity and impulsivity. But these basic symptoms can have ramifications across the spectrum of work duties—in Audra's case, with memory, focusing, prioritizing, organizing, and multitasking. As can be common in adults with ADHD, Audra had some accompanying psychological difficulties, symptoms of both depression and anxiety that made it even more difficult for her to cope. Most adults have demands outside of their work, such as children, spouses, or outside activities and organizations. But in Audra's case, the increased demands of taking care of her parents overwhelmed her ability to cope. The added time needed to complete the tasks required by her job left her little time for attending to other responsibilities in her life.

 GETTING BACK ON TRACK

In the following sections, we cover three areas that will help you be more successful at work. The first step in getting back on track is to choose a job or career that is a good fit for you, given your particular ADHD symptoms as well as your overall profile. Next, we discuss ways to cope with distractibility and lack of focus during your workday. Third, we talk about your legal rights to specific accommodations at work.

CHOOSING A JOB THAT WORKS FOR YOU

Understand Yourself

The first step is to have a very thorough evaluation of your ADHD so that you understand your particular symptoms, as well as your strengths and weaknesses. Symptoms of primarily inattention will present very different difficulties from those presented by symptoms of hyperactivity or impulsivity. Using the two checklists on pp. 188–189, first rate all the things you do well in your job. Follow this up with a rating of the things that are more difficult for you.

> Online inventories and websites such as http://www.self-directed-search.com and http://www.mynextmove.org can be helpful tools in your career matching process.

Things I Do Well at Work

☐ Arrive on time

☐ Follow directions

☐ Complete what I'm supposed to each day

☐ Pay attention during meetings

☐ Get along well with my coworkers

☐ Get along well with my boss or supervisor

☐ Think creatively

☐ Have a positive attitude

☐ Try my best

☐ Am persistent in completing tasks

☐ Have a good memory

☐ Rarely take a sick day

☐ Am a team player

☐ Am honest and can be trusted

☐ Am organized

☐ Am good at dealing with the public or with customers

☐ Have good telephone skills

☐ Have good computer skills

☐ Do what I'm told without complaint

☐ Can work independently

☐ Am organized and can find things when needed

☐ Don't give up easily

☐ Don't mind putting in long hours

☐ Understand how to do my job. I have the skills and knowledge I need

☐ Really enjoy what I do

☐ Am a self-starter

☐ Enjoy new challenges

Write below other things that you do well:

_____ _____ _____

_____ _____ _____

_____ _____ _____

Things I Have Difficulty With at Work

☐ Frequently late for work

☐ Frequently late for meetings

☐ Forget to show up for meetings

☐ Don't get my work done on time

☐ Often behind in my work

☐ Takes me longer than my coworkers to get the same things done

☐ Get bored easily

☐ Get distracted easily

☐ Lose focus

☐ Can't work very long at one time on one thing

☐ Lose track of what I'm supposed to be doing

☐ Find it hard to concentrate on my work

☐ Have a difficult time prioritizing my job duties

☐ Don't have the skills or knowledge to do my job

☐ Not a self-starter

☐ Don't get along well with my coworkers

☐ Don't get along well my boss

☐ Am moody

☐ Don't work well in groups

☐ Get in arguments a lot

☐ Really dislike my job

☐ Don't take feedback well

☐ Don't like someone telling me what to do

☐ Wish I had a different job

Write below other things you have difficulty with:

_____ _____ _____

_____ _____ _____

_____ _____ _____

These charts are a good place to start as you put together a profile of yourself as a worker. Try to categorize your strengths and weaknesses. Can you see patterns in the areas of interpersonal skills, attitude and initiative, organizational skills, time management, or work ethic? Try to categorize the individual questions into these areas. You will need to add some other information to round this out. At this stage you may need to visit to a psychologist, career counselor, ADHD coach, or other professional, as some of the following information may be best obtained with standardized tests.

The following worksheet will give you a place to start thinking, keep track, and organize your work profile.

My Work Profile

Past History. List here facts about your past education and jobs. These should include subjects you liked or did well at, subjects you did poorly in, previous jobs you've had, likes or dislikes regarding those jobs, and previous accomplishments or successes.

_____

_____

_____

_____

Skills and Aptitudes. List here particular things you do well, such as computer skills, artistic or musical ability, working with numbers, reading, working with people, or building things.

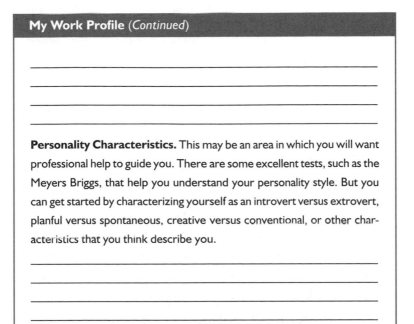

My Work Profile (*Continued*)

_____

_____

_____

_____

Personality Characteristics. This may be an area in which you will want professional help to guide you. There are some excellent tests, such as the Meyers Briggs, that help you understand your personality style. But you can get started by characterizing yourself as an introvert versus extrovert, planful versus spontaneous, creative versus conventional, or other characteristics that you think describe you.

_____

_____

_____

_____

Consider Your Job Match

With these pieces of information in hand, you are ready to determine whether there is a good match between your current job and the profile you have put together. Is your current situation well suited to your strengths? If your match indicates a poor fit, can you create a better match by gaining some additional skills, changing your job duties somewhat, or just engaging in an attitude adjustment? If you conclude that you will continue to feel like a square peg in a round hole, then you should seriously consider working with a career counselor to

Good-fit careers for adults with ADHD:

- Sales
- Teaching
- Acting
- Marketing
- Art

change your career path. If you are still in school and still considering your major or career goals, now is an excellent time to go through this exercise. It is very common for college students with ADHD to have an unrealistic view of their suitability for their chosen major. However, if you have long been out of school and in your current field, it is not too late. Many times decisions are made on the basis of parental pressure, current trends (business, medicine, and law seem to be popular choices), or merely "falling" into a major without careful thought or planning. For some people, many careers can be rewarding and doable, but for adults with ADHD, it is imperative to select a job or career that fits your particular needs. In the case study of Audra, her current job was a very poor match on the basis of her symptoms of ADHD. Her job required many skills that are difficult for adults with ADHD, such as attention to detail, good memory, ability to plan and stick to a schedule, and the ability to focus.

Although your job choice needs to be made on the basis of your particular profile, many experts suggest that adults with ADHD should avoid jobs that include sitting at a desk all day and involve repetitive, detail-oriented work. More suitable jobs might be ones that involve creativity, spontaneity, the ability to set your own hours, and a degree of variety. But be careful about selecting a job with too much flexibility; some adults with ADHD need clear deadlines and someone to hold them accountable. Otherwise, their tendency to procrastinate may prevent them from following through on tasks. Some good job choices for adults with ADHD might include teaching, sales, or marketing. Managerial or administrative jobs might be quite suitable if there are support staff who take care of structure, organization, and day-to-day details. Many adults with ADHD become entrepreneurs and are quite successful. Adults with ADHD can thrive in jobs that allow them to plan, create new endeavors, solicit contracts, and envision the big picture. Then, they turn the implementation and monitoring over to their detail-oriented support staff. Other jobs may not be an ideal fit but can be made more manageable if one has an understanding boss and supportive coworkers.

BEING MORE EFFECTIVE ON THE JOB

Organization and Time Management

These two skills are critical to being an effective employee. That's why we devoted entire chapters to each of these topics; therefore, we won't review these topics again here. Be sure to review them (Chapter 5 on organization and Chapter 3 on time management), as they complement the other topics included in this chapter.

Overcoming Distractibility and Lack of Focus

After organization and time-management skills, the third most important aspect of your workday will be maintaining your focus throughout the day. If you have a diagnosis of ADHD, it is probably difficult for you to put in an 8-hour day while maintaining maximum concentration. It may be hard for you to do this for even 30 minutes.

This section goes over some key concepts to help you spend as much of your workday as possible actually working.

First, it's important that you at least consider medication. Research has suggested that the primary benefit of medication is that it allows you to focus. If you are not on medication, or it does not seem to be working for you, you might want to skip ahead and review Chapter 9 on medication.

There are numerous coping strategies to help you focus. A good place to start is making your physical environment less distracting. Consider your work space. Are there ways you can reduce noise and traffic flow? You might have a private office, a cubicle, or work on your feet most of the day. Regardless of your circumstances, spend some time evaluating your environment and work with your supervisor to make any helpful structural changes you can to your physical space. If physical changes are not possible, can you vary your work hours so that you are able to come in early or work late, when other people are not around? A white noise machine is fairly inexpensive and can block out a good deal of noise when it's not possible to change your physical setting.

Next, consider the types of things that distract you. Check any of the following that apply:

☐ People interrupting with questions specifically for me

☐ People interrupting with nonessential information, gossip, or just being noisy within hearing distance

☐ Interrupting others to avoid doing work or to seek stimulation

☐ Telephone

☐ E-mail

☐ My thoughts

☐ Other _____

Each of these will require different solutions, but the more distractions you can identify and treat, the more efficient you will become. If other people interrupt you, work with your boss and colleagues to determine whether your job requires that you be available at all times for things that "come up." Is there an expectation that you will be available on an immediate basis? If not, are you allowed to close your door or put up a "Do Not Disturb" sign during specified times when you are working on tasks?

If responding to your phone and e-mail get you off task, can you turn off your ringer, let your voicemail pick up, and select certain times during the day to listen and respond to messages? The same goes for e-mail. Even those with the best of intentions can spend all day long just responding to e-mail. Can you train yourself to check your e-mail at specified times? This method for both phone and e-mail can also work as a type of reward to keep you on track with other tasks ("I'll work solidly on this report for 45 minutes and then check my phone and e-mail as a way of taking a break"). Remember, a task doesn't necessarily have to be "fun" to qualify as a reward; sometimes it just has to be different. Some adults with ADHD can work for long periods of time, as long as the actual tasks have variety.

If your distractions occur inside your head, you will need an outlet to keep yourself from jumping from one task to another. Keep a small notebook or list handy. When intrusive thoughts about other things you need to be doing pop into your head, jot them down and promise to add them to your to-do list later. Do not give in and work on them right away unless they are true emergencies. Some adults find it helpful to set a small timer to go off at regular short intervals, such as every 10 minutes. When the timer rings, they mark down whether or not they are actually focusing on a task. If their mind has begun to wander, the timer is a reminder that helps to bring them back to the task at hand. The timer also gradually conditions them to be more aware of when and how their mind wanders and can eventually be discontinued when this process becomes more under their conscious control.

WORKPLACE ACCOMMODATIONS FOR ADHD

If you have followed the suggestions above about choosing a job that works for you and implementing good coping strategies, this next section will hopefully be unnecessary. However, if you find that your current employment is negatively impacted by your symptoms of ADHD, read on. One of the major decisions you will need to make is whether to disclose to your employer that you have ADHD. You might do this somewhat informally at first. For example, suggest to your boss that you know from past experience that you work best under certain circumstances, such as when you take frequent breaks, have a work space that is free from distractions, or have all assignments written down and sent over e-mail. Try to approach this from a position of strength. Have a discussion early on with your supervisor about ways you know that you work well, and don't wait until you have problems and it comes across as an excuse. Many supervisors are happy to make changes that facilitate your efficiency. You might need to help educate your employer about ADHD. It may be helpful to print out descriptions of ADHD from one of the numerous websites mentioned in this book. Some employers will be more willing to listen to your suggestions if they learn more about ADHD from a credible source.

Alternatively, you can make a formal disclosure of your ADHD with documentation of your diagnosis and, if necessary, refer to legally mandated protections that you are entitled to under the Americans With Disabilities Act (ADA) of 1990. This federal law gives you specific protections and prevents employers from discriminating against you. The ADA is periodically amended, such as in 2008, so it's a good idea to check the government website (http://www.ada.gov/newregs.htm) to see what might be new. The ADA will cover you if you work for a private employer who has 15 or more employees; an entity of the federal, state, and local governments, including those receiving federal funds; employment agencies and labor organizations; and "places of public accommodation," including most private schools and higher education institutions.

According to the ADA, if you want to receive certain accommodations at work, you must disclose to your employer that you have a disability, which generally means that you must include some type of documentation. A diagnosis of ADHD does not automatically qualify you for accommodations; it depends on the circumstances. You will likely need a current evaluation report written by a licensed psychologist or physician that specifically states what limitations you have. This report will need to show that you have a physical or mental impairment that causes substantial limitations in a major life activity. You have to be otherwise qualified for the job; for example, you can't claim ADHD as a reason for being denied a job in a biology lab if you were an English major with no biology experience or expertise.

Employers are only required to make reasonable accommodations to help you perform your work duties. For example, they might be required to let you use a tape recorder in meetings but not be required to provide someone to take notes for you. They might be required to give you a work space that is not overly distracting but not be required to give you a private office if all other workers have cubicles. They might be required to let you use noise-blocking earphones during the day but not if that prevents you from hearing the phone ring and your primary job is as a receptionist. You might be allowed a 10-minute break every hour if you make up the time by working longer each day but not if your job is as a nurse in an emergency room and that 10-minute break would put patients at risk. You might be allowed to take an hour off each week to attend ADHD coaching sessions but not to take a 20-hour per week position that you think is more flexible. There are no hard and fast rules about what is reasonable. Initially, it's up to you to meet with your employer and together brainstorm solutions that might be mutually agreeable. If the employer can show that the accommodations would create an undue hardship, he or she doesn't have to make them.

If you feel you are being treated unfairly because of your symptoms of ADHD and that your employer is violating the ADA, you might want to consider filing a complaint with the Equal

Employment Opportunity Commission (EEOC), the federal agency that enforces the ADA and other civil rights laws. The EEOC's telephone number is 1-800-669-4000. The time frame for filing is different in different states, and it can vary from 180 to 300 days from the date of the alleged discrimination, so be sure to check the requirements where you live. There is no cost to file a complaint, and you are not required to have a lawyer. After you file a complaint, the EEOC will notify your employer that a charge has been filed. There are several possible outcomes. The EEOC might investigate and determine that your charge is groundless, they might require that you enter into mediation (a free service that involves an impartial third person who listens to you both and helps you to come to an agreement), they might decide that you have been treated unfairly and work with your employer to make accommodations, or they might initiate a lawsuit against your employer.

As you can see, this can become fairly complicated, so it's a good idea to think very carefully about whether you want to pursue this option. Sometimes you can win a case but be in a job situation that is so stressful that you dread going to work each day. Hopefully, you can avoid ever having to take this step by carefully selecting a job or career up front that works for you and by learning on your own how to be organized, practice good time management, and reduce distractibility.

There are many common coping techniques suggested by both experts in the field and adult workers who have a diagnosis of ADHD. The tips below are a compilation of these suggestions and can be helpful as easy reminders.

TRY IT! HELPFUL TIPS FOR IMPROVING WORK PERFORMANCE

1. Use a daily planner that also has a long-term (week or month) view. Highlight important dates, meetings, and deadlines. Supplement with reminders on a whiteboard, in your phone, or through another system that works for you.

2. Develop a system to accommodate your restlessness. Build in physical activity all day long, such as taking the stairs, incorporating short exercise breaks in your office, walking to the copy room, or volunteering to do minor errands. Try to leave the office during lunch.

3. Develop a system to accommodate your boredom. Reward yourself on a set schedule (at least once an hour) with something enjoyable (read a few pages of a novel, surf the Internet, have a snack, do some exercise, make a phone call).

4. Develop a system for prioritizing your day (rate your tasks A, B, C; list them in order, or give them stars). Stick to this priority list. Repeat this daily.

5. Consider using a set time each day to open mail, answer e-mail, or complete other tasks that tend to distract you.

6. Break your larger tasks into smaller units, preferably things that can be accomplished in less than an hour. It will help you to be able to mark these off as you accomplish them, rather than feel overwhelmed by a job that takes several days to complete.

7. When you are distracted by the thought of a task other than the one you're doing, write it down but resist the

urge to do the other task right away. Wait until you have finished the task you're working on.

8. Develop a system for organizing your space. Have a place for everything (papers, pens, books, work to do, completed work). Use labels, files, or baskets. Always put things in their place as soon as possible. Learn to throw things away.

9. Stay focused in meetings by taking notes and asking questions. Bring a small object to manipulate in your hands to help with your need to fidget.

10. Use a phone, clock, or timer to ring an alarm 5 minutes before you need to be somewhere.

11. Use some of the functions on your smartphone, such as an electronic calendar or a system that rings or notifies you of appointments or deadlines.

12. Always carry a small notebook for reminders. Transfer these to your scheduler as soon as possible.

13. When having conversations, try to repeat back or paraphrase what is being said. This helps you focus, helps you remember, and lets the other person know you are interested and paying attention.

14. Ask your boss or colleagues to put requests in writing. Make sure that you understand what is to be done and that you know the due date.

15. Create self-imposed deadlines for tasks. Many adults with ADHD report that they are motivated by deadlines and tend to procrastinate unless they have a specific time constraint.

16. Take time at the end of each day to straighten, file, and organize. It's much easier to get started the next day if you come in to an organized office.

17. Try to incorporate daily exercise, meditation, relaxation, or deep breathing into your routine.

SUMMARY

To summarize, here are the important points you will want to take away from this chapter. Use the following checklist to note the areas you have thoroughly studied. Leave the box empty if it is an area you would like to come back to and review further.

☐ I understand how ADHD symptoms play out in the workplace.

☐ I have learned how to choose a job that works for me.

☐ I have learned ways to be more effective on the job.

☐ I understand how to seek accommodations from my employer if work problems persist.

Part III

GETTING ADDITIONAL HELP

 Part III of this book focuses on next steps in terms of finding the best treatment for you and your specific struggles related to adult ADHD. You may have coexisting anxiety or depression that warrants help that is outside the scope of this book. Or you may be interested in learning about your options in terms of medication, counseling, or natural ways to improve your overall functioning. Specifically, here are the important lessons you will want to take away from Part III:

- How to better understand conditions like depression, anxiety, and learning disabilities, which often coexist with ADHD.
- How to navigate the complex world of medication options for ADHD.
- How to understand your options for treatment, then locate and select the course of treatment that is right for you.
- How to overcome any lingering fears you may have of asking for or receiving professional help.

CHAPTER EIGHT

UNDERSTANDING AND TREATING CONDITIONS THAT CAN COEXIST WITH ADHD

Stress is when you wake up screaming, and then realize that you haven't fallen asleep yet.
—Author Unknown

The term *comorbidity* is used in psychology to indicate that you have one disorder and, at the same time, you have a second, different disorder. Usually, the two disorders are thought to be unrelated to one another, like having a cold at the same time that you have poison ivy. Having the cold is totally unrelated to the fact that you walked in the woods and picked up poison ivy. But even though they are unrelated, your suffering is increased because you have two different sets of symptoms at one time.

With ADHD, comorbidity means that you have both ADHD and one or more other mental health issues going on simultaneously.

The challenge can be to figure out what different diagnoses you actually qualify for and how they may be related. Let's say your primary symptom is lack of concentration. That can be a symptom of ADHD, or of depression, or of anxiety. It's possible that you have one of those disorders, or two, or even all three. It's possible that you started as a child with ADHD, and then because of your symptoms, you were constantly getting in trouble, which then caused you to become depressed about your life. Additionally, not doing well in school may have caused you some test anxiety and worry about your schoolwork. So you might have a situation in which the ADHD came first and actually caused the comorbid conditions. Or it's possible that you have ADHD and depression and anxiety all at the same time, but they're totally unrelated to one another. You can see how figuring out what might be going on can get tricky. But it's important to have a clear picture of your diagnoses so that your treatment is appropriate. Sometimes alleviating the symptoms of one problem makes the other problems go away, and other times you need to independently treat everything. In this chapter, we discuss some common comorbid conditions and give suggestions for how you might deal with them.

WHAT THE EXPERTS SAY: COMMON COMORBIDITIES WITH ADHD

Some of our best information about comorbid disorders comes from research done at Harvard Medical School. Researchers there conducted two very large surveys: the National Comorbidity Survey, in the early 1990s, and the National Comorbidity Survey Replication,

10 years later. Researchers did intensive interviews with 10,000 people to find out what mental health and substance abuse problems tend to occur together. They found that adults with ADHD had numerous comorbid mental health disorders. The most common were an anxiety disorder (47% of the adults with ADHD also had anxiety), a mood disorder such as depression or bipolar disorder (38%), an impulse control disorder such as intermittent explosive disorder (19%), or a substance disorder such as drug or alcohol abuse or dependence (15%). Other researchers have looked at many more possible mental health problems and found that adults with ADHD also have significant comorbidity with oppositional defiant disorder, conduct disorder, personality disorders, sleep problems, learning disabilities, and autism spectrum disorders.

Researchers have estimated that between 65% and 89% of all individuals with ADHD will have one or more additional mental health disorders. More than 45% of adults with ADHD will have two or more comorbid mental health disorders. Again, the most common will be anxiety disorders and depression. There is also some evidence that agoraphobia (a complication of panic attacks and fear of public places) might be a common comorbidity.

In general, it's somewhat disappointing to realize that having a second disorder at some time during your life appears to be the norm rather than the exception. So, it's really important to look out for these symptoms, catch them early, and ask your doctor or psychologist for help in treating them. You don't want your symptoms of ADHD to be even more difficult to contend with because the long-term effects of other symptoms are making them worse. How can you avoid this? There are some important things to watch out for.

The wrong diagnosis can lead to the wrong medication. If you are being treated for ADHD and are on medication but your comorbid depression is undiagnosed, your doctor may think the ADHD medication isn't working because you might still be distracted or unable to concentrate. But this could be due to depression, not to the ADHD. So you might go through several months of trying out ADHD medications that don't seem to work when actually you need to be using medication(s) designed for both ADHD and depression. So it's extremely important to have proper diagnoses to make sure you are medicating the right disorder.

The wrong diagnosis can mean some symptoms remain untreated. On the other hand, suppose you have been diagnosed with anxiety or depression. There are some good, effective treatments for those. But if you have ADHD and don't know it, your progress can be greatly hindered until you treat all of your symptoms. Think back to our example of having a cold and poison ivy. Suppose you thought you only had a cold, and you attributed your itchiness to the cold, so you took only an antihistamine and a decongestant. You might stop sneezing and coughing, but your itch would probably get worse, and you wouldn't feel much better overall until you put some lotion on the poison ivy rash.

The wrong diagnosis can make your symptoms worse. Finally, there are some instances in which the medication you might take for ADHD actually makes other undiagnosed disorders worse. The best-known case of this type occurs when a specialist treats a person's ADHD with a stimulant, not realizing that the person also has an anxiety disorder. It's possible that the stimulant medication can actually make the person's anxiety much worse. So, in summary, it's crucially important that you understand how disorders co-occur, that you keep an eye out for signs that you might have more than ADHD going on, and that you get good treatment that fits with your particular configuration.

In the following sections, we give you some in-depth information on the two most common comorbidities with ADHD: anxiety and depression. For each of these, we start with some easy questions to give you a "heads up" that you might want to pursue this further with your doctor, psychologist, or counselor. Then we describe the disorder in detail and end with some suggestions about what you might do if you have comorbid anxiety or depression.

Be strongly advised that the material presented in this chapter does not make you an expert and should in no way help you to self-diagnose. Furthermore, even if you answer all the questions positively, it doesn't mean you have another disorder. Instead, should any of the material ring true for you, it just means you might want monitor yourself and definitely discuss any concerns with your doctor or psychologist.

 ANXIETY

The list of questions that follow can give you an idea of whether anxiety may be affecting you. There are many types of anxiety, so we have arranged the questions into four categories.

Category A

1. Have you had, on more than one occasion, four or more of the following symptoms all at once: pounding heart,

sweating, trembling, shortness of breath, feeling like you are choking, chest discomfort, nausea, dizziness or feeling faint, fear of losing control, fear of dying, numbness or tingling, chills or hot flashes?

2. If you have had the group of symptoms above, do you worry a lot about having this happen again?

Category B

1. Do you worry about social situations with people you don't know because you think you might embarrass yourself?
2. Do you avoid social situations with people you don't know?
3. Do social situations with people you don't know make you anxious?

Category C

1. Do you get anxious when you are taking a test or being evaluated?
2. Do you get anxious just studying for a class or preparing for an evaluation?

Category D

1. Do you worry consistently about a number of things, such as work or school or life in general?
2. Do you find it difficult to control your worry?
3. When you worry, does it include three or more of the following: restlessness, fatigue, difficulty concentrating, irritability, muscle tension, sleep problems?

Key to Categories

You will see that the four categories tap into somewhat different types of worry or anxiety. (There are actually more types of anxiety, but the four we are covering are the most common ones.) You should let your physician or psychologist know if you answered "yes" to all of the questions within a single category.

Category A inquires about panic attacks. These involve a very specific but short period of time in which you have very intense fear or discomfort. During this time you have numerous physical symptoms, such as pounding heart, sweating, trembling, or shortness of breath. You feel like you really want to escape from wherever you are, and in severe cases, you might be fearful that you are dying, going crazy, or having a heart attack. Panic attacks can be unexpected and totally out of the blue, or they can be associated with specific events, like going to the doctor or public speaking. One of the worst things about panic attacks can be the subsequent worry about having another one.

Category B relates to social anxiety. This means you worry about being in situations or with people because you think you are going to do something to really embarrass yourself. So you either avoid people and situations entirely or you grit your teeth and get through them with a great deal of dread and apprehension, and you certainly don't enjoy the experience. You can see how this would make it hard to go to a party, stand up in class and answer questions, or even give a presentation at work.

Category C focuses on test anxiety. In the work we do with college students, we find that test anxiety is the most common form of anxiety associated with ADHD. This seems to be the case because the symptoms of ADHD (disorganization, lack of concentration, forgetfulness) are often associated with poor study skills. Therefore, many students with ADHD have test anxiety because they have had a difficult time preparing for a test, are often not ready, know from past experience that they will run out of time, and know that they will have difficulty concentrating during the test. So their test anxiety

> **The four most common types of anxiety that co-occur with adult ADHD:**
> - Test anxiety
> - Generalized anxiety
> - Social anxiety
> - Panic attacks

is very realistic because of their past performance. This can also affect you in your job if you worry about assignments or presentations and get anxious when you have a specific task coming up.

Category D is for generalized anxiety. With generalized anxiety you tend to worry almost every day about a variety of things, and you just can't seem to get a handle on your worry or overcome it. You may worry about your job, finances, kids, your marriage, or car repairs; it just seems like you are in a constant, low-level state of anxiety.

What To Do About Anxiety

First, write down the things that you seem to worry about on the lines below. Try to rank them, with #1 being your top worry.

1. _____
2. _____

3. _____

4. _____

5. _____

Second, consider whether these are things you can address on your own or whether you may require the help of a professional. There are a lot of effective treatments for anxiety. If your worries seem to be directly related to your symptoms of ADHD, then you might consider ADHD coaching or just trying some of the suggestions in this book. For example, are you worried about studying and taking tests (Chapter 6), your job performance (Chapter 7), your relationships with others (Chapter 4), or always being disorganized and feeling overwhelmed (Chapter 2)? Many of the suggestions in this book will help you deal directly with your symptoms, and your anxiety may be reduced as you learn better ways to deal with your symptoms of ADHD. If you have panic attacks or just seem overwhelmed by your worries, you might consider seeing a psychologist. There are some specific treatments that involve teaching you how to relax, developing a hierarchy of your fears and helping you face them one by one, using self-talk to counteract your negative thoughts, or just gaining insight into the nature of your fears and coming up with specific strategies to cope with them. If you are on medication for your ADHD, you should talk with your physician because you will likely benefit from medication that targets both your ADHD symptoms and your anxiety.

Finally, go back and review the things that make you worried or anxious. Do they seem to be stress related? Are you just overwhelmed by having too much to do in your life? Many of the clients we see are stressed out because their symptoms of ADHD (poor organization, forgetfulness, poor planning, chronic lateness) cause them to be constantly doing things at the last minute. They wind up skipping appointments, classes, or events because they are behind on some other activity, which puts them behind on the activity they skipped. Again, it's a vicious cycle.

HELP YOURSELF! DECREASE ANXIETY BY REDUCING STRESS

Although anxiety and stress are two different things, we often find that reducing stress in your life can reduce your anxiety also. Sometimes you are stressed because your priorities are out of whack and you spend too much time doing things that you don't want to be doing. Let's see if you can identify some ways that your time might be out of balance. Fill in the chart below, listing the amount of time you actually spend in different activities and then the amount of time you would *like* to be spending in those activities.

Ways You Spend Your Time			
Ways you spend your time	How many hours per week (based on 100) do you *currently* devote to this?	How many hours per week (based on 100) would you *like* to devote to this?	Check here if there's more than a 5-hour difference in your two columns
Work			
School and studying			
Time with family			
Exercise			
Fun/social/ entertainment			

Ways You Spend Your Time *(Continued)*			
Ways you spend your time	How many hours per week (based on 100) do you *currently* devote to this?	How many hours per week (based on 100) would you *like* to devote to this?	Check here if there's more than a 5-hour difference in your two columns
Personal (reading, TV, computer)			
Church/volunteer/ organizations			
Other (list)			

How many checks did you have in the last column? Think carefully about those activities. Can you say NO to anything you're doing too much of? Can you include more of the activities that you want to be doing? Pick one of the activities that seems out of whack and make a conscious decision to rebalance. Set a goal for yourself over the next few weeks of changing the amount of time you're spending on the activity you've selected.

 GETTING BACK ON TRACK: A STRATEGY TO REDUCE YOUR GENERAL ANXIETY

Some days, or in some situations, you just feel anxious. It might be due to an upcoming evaluation, or a talk you have to give, or a social situation, or perhaps you can't identify a reason—you just feel anxious. For generalized anxiety, many psychologists use a technique called *progressive relaxation*. There are many variations of this technique, and you can adapt it to fit your own needs. You can spend 30 minutes doing this, or do a shortened version in 5 minutes.

Find a quiet spot where you can dim the lights and you are not distracted by noise. Sit in as comfortable a position as possible. One variation is to have quiet meditational music in the background, but you can do progressive relaxation with or without this. Close your eyes. Take a few minutes to let your thoughts flow freely. Imagine these thoughts draining out of your mind or floating off in the wind or simply becoming smaller and smaller. Take deep breaths, if it's comfortable for you, and try to breathe in through your nose and out through your mouth. Try to breathe deeply into your abdomen. Imagine your abdomen is a tire or a balloon and each breath slowly fills it up. Some people do better if they count slowly 1-2-3-4 as they inhale and then 1-2-3-4 as they exhale. Take a few minutes just to slow your breathing. Now concentrate on your left hand. Clench your fist. Feel the tightness. Hold for a few seconds and then relax it. Feel it going loose and wiggle your fingers. Imagine your fingers feeling heavy and needing to rest on your leg. Repeat. If you have intrusive thoughts as you do this, don't worry; let them flow through your mind and out. Push them out slowly with your breathing. You will usually find that if you are concentrating on your breathing and relaxing, there is not much space left for other thoughts. Now move up your arm, repeating the process with your elbow, your shoulders, your neck. When you do your neck, roll your head around after tensing your neck, feeling it very heavy and wanting to flop over. Repeat with your jaw, and then your facial muscles. Now go to your toes, ankle, then lower and upper legs, then lower back and buttocks. When you have tensed and released all your major muscles (or as much as you have time for), slump and relax your whole body for a minute.

Focus on your breathing, counting 1-2-3-4 as you inhale and exhale. Imagine all the tension flowing from your body. Finish by standing and gently stretching. Once you get the hang of this it becomes easier and easier, and your body seems to automatically go through the steps.

Go back up to your list of worries. Was work one of them? If so, you might find the following 10 easy ways to reduce stress at work helpful:

1. Make your relationship with your boss a top priority. Do what it takes to get along with him or her; it will make your life infinitely better!
2. Avoid drinking coffee all day long. Try to substitute water or reduced sugar fruit juice.
3. Write a priority list every day. Don't put too much on it. Make it manageable.
4. Try to make your work space pleasant. Hang some pictures, buy a small throw rug, or bring in a plant.
5. Always try to take a lunch break. If you bring your own lunch, go outside or meet with a friend.
6. Take a couple of 10-minute exercise breaks each day; do yoga, go for a walk, or do some stretches.
7. Build pleasant, cooperative relationships with as many of your coworkers as possible.
8. Figure out ways to reduce distracting noise. Use a fan, a white noise machine, or low background music, or ask to move your office.

9. Learn to ignore, delegate, or procrastinate when faced with trivia. Trivia can eat up your time, but if left alone, it often goes away.

10. Learn when it's OK to give less than 100% effort on a task. Sometimes that last 10% takes up hours of time, and 90% would have been just fine for that particular activity.

DEPRESSION

The second most common comorbidity with ADHD is depression. There are many levels of depression, ranging from mild feelings to something that can become life threatening. As with anxiety, there are many things you can do to avoid or lessen depression. The first is to be aware of the symptoms. Take the miniquiz below to see if you may be struggling with symptoms of depression.

Category A

1. Do you often have problems with your appetite—either you overeat, or you don't feel like eating at all?

2. Do you often have problems sleeping—either you can't sleep, or you want to sleep all the time?

3. Are you often tired or have no energy?

4. Do you have low self-esteem?

5. Do you find it hard to make decisions?

6. Do you feel hopeless?

7. Do you feel sad or empty?

8. Do you have little interest in doing things?
9. Do you feel worthless or guilty?

Category B

1. Do you think about dying a lot or think about suicide?

Key to Categories

You should contact a psychologist or physician if you answered "yes" to four or more of the questions in Category A or if you answered "yes" to the single question in Category B. Again, keep in mind that this quiz is not meant to let you to self-diagnose. And even if you answer all the questions positively, it doesn't mean you are clinically depressed. It just means you might want to keep an eye on this and mention it to your doctor or psychologist.

Category A represents common symptoms of depression. It's very normal to have some of the symptoms from Category A and to feel depressed sometimes. It can be a problem if you experience *many* of these symptoms, a *great deal* of the time, over a *long period* of time, at a fairly high level of *intensity*, to such a degree that it really begins to *negatively impact* your school, or your work, your social relationships, or your ability to enjoy life. Similar to anxiety, sometimes you need to work with a psychologist or see a psychiatrist for medication. However, just like anxiety, there are also some things you can do on your own.

Category B indicates you may be severely depressed and in need of immediate professional help. Suicidal thoughts are not something to be taken lightly. If you answered yes to this question you should put down this book and contact someone now.

HELP YOURSELF! DEVELOP A BLUES BUSTER LIST

Many times you can catch yourself sliding into a period of sadness or depression. Try to recognize the signs and be prepared to stop the cycle before it starts. Have on hand a list of proven strategies for you that typically perk you up. For example, buy a book you've wanted to read, a DVD you've wanted to watch, or take on a craft activity you've wanted to work on. Set the list aside and only take it out when you really need a Blues Buster. Plan a project (build something, plant something, paint something). Set aside a recipe you've wanted to make. Buy something (a new shirt, a pair of running shoes), but leave it in the bag. Keep a list of rewarding charitable organizations (Habitat for Humanity, your local food pantry or homeless shelter) that you've been meaning to volunteer for, and have their phone numbers handy. Plan to visit a new store or museum or restaurant, but don't go there yet.

Save these activities, but keep the list handy so that when you need an immediate pick-me-up, you don't get bogged down in trying to think of something or don't have the energy to get it started. Just go to your list and pick one! Write down some ideas for your list below. During the next month, complete your Blues Buster list and have it ready when needed.

Blues Buster Ideas		
Idea	What I need to do/ buy to get it ready	Check off here when its ready
1.		
2.		
3.		
4.		
5.		
6.		
7.		
8.		
9.		
10.		

In addition to having your Blues Buster plan in place, the following tips are some fairly simple things you can do to avoid or reduce minor depression:

1. Follow our earlier suggestions for a healthy lifestyle and reducing stress. There is scientific proof that poor diet and exercise are linked to depression. Stress is also a major cause of depression.

2. Reach out to others by taking a class, joining a club, joining an online chat group, or renewing your contact with relatives. Social contact is an important component in alleviating depression. Isolation and loneliness generally make depression worse.

3. Keep a journal of positive affirmations. Each day, write down something you are thankful for or something positive about yourself or your life.

4. Volunteer. Use the Internet to search the word volunteer and then the name of your city and state. You'll probably get well over a hundred possibilities.

5. Make a plan for something you want to do. Having something to look forward to helps in two ways. One, the actual planning is enjoyable and keeps you busy. Two, the anticipation of the event can be exciting. So plan a trip or vacation or activity.

6. Change your attitude for just one day. Get out of bed and say thank you for being alive. Expect a good day. When the first complaint enters your head, think of a way to improve the situation. Smile at least three times, at something in particular or for no reason at all. Say thank you to someone, with feeling. Pay a compliment to someone during the day. If someone greets you with, "Hi, how are you?" respond with "I'm great!" and then make some positive comment about the day or the weather or the world.

If You Need More Help

Sometimes, attempts to overcome depression by yourself are just not enough. You may want to consult a psychiatrist for medication or a psychologist for therapy. The good news is that depression is a disorder for which there are scientifically proven treatment methods. The most common therapy for depression is called *cognitive–behavioral therapy*

(CBT). CBT combines two approaches: the cognitive part works on changing how you think about yourself, while the behavioral part teaches to actually alter your behaviors. Thoughts and behaviors can have a snowball effect. If you think more positive thoughts, you tend to act differently, both on your own and toward those around you. These positive actions make you feel better and also cause other people to respond to you more positively. So then you start interpreting things differently and view the world more positively, and then you behave differently . . . and so it goes in an upward spiral. This type of therapy is quite successful and relatively short term. You can expect to see changes in a matter of months. You can find more on CBT and other therapeutic interventions in Chapter 10.

BIPOLAR DISORDER

A different type of depression that you also want to be aware of is called *bipolar disorder*. This condition combines the features of depression that we've just discussed with an elevated or manic phase. The two conditions occur in an episodic way, such that you might have a period of days or weeks in which you have the symptoms of depression, followed by a period in which you go through a manic phase. The manic phase is characterized by being overly talkative and distractible, with increased activity, physical restlessness, and loss of social inhibition. Sound familiar? These manic symptoms are similar to symptoms of ADHD, which is why ADHD and bipolar disorder are frequently confused or misdiagnosed. Fortunately, there are some additional symptoms of the manic phase that are not typical of ADHD. These are significantly decreased need for sleep, very unusual thoughts or even hallucinations, and greatly inflated self-esteem. Also, if you have ADHD, you tend to have the same symptoms consistently across time, whereas if you have bipolar disorder there is more of a periodic nature to your symptoms. But the distinction between the two is not always clear. For example, one of our clients came in thinking that he had ADHD. This older gentleman had been married twice and reported always having difficulty in relationships. He had held numerous jobs and couldn't seem to settle on a career. He reported having over 30 parking tickets and numerous driving citations. He had never done well in school, although he did better in subjects that he liked. At this point it sounded as if he might meet the criteria for ADHD. However, he went on to say that he rarely slept more than 3 hours a night and would go through phases during which he would stay up for 2 days to work on a project that was going to "change his life." He would then "crash" and spend a week or two not wanting to get out of bed and feeling angry and resentful toward the world. This information led to a diagnosis of bipolar disorder. Bipolar disorder is difficult to treat on your own without the help of a psychiatrist or psychologist, so if you think this description may fit you, it's a good idea to seek outside help.

WARNING: MEDICATION AND COMORBID DISORDERS

There are a couple of cautions you need to be aware of if you are taking, or plan to take, medication for ADHD, anxiety, depression, or bipolar disorder, in addition to thoroughly reading Chapter 9, in which medication options are covered in more detail. However, for the time being, just keep in mind that many symptoms and disorders are related and that the medications you take might interact. For example, some research has shown that a stimulant used to control ADHD symptoms might make anxiety symptoms worse. Stimulants can also make the manic phases of bipolar disorder worse. There are nonstimulant medications for ADHD that might be a better choice, as they can simultaneously help multiple symptoms. Some experts have suggested that you try to judge which disorder causes the most impairment and treat that first with medication before considering other medications for less impairing disorders.

CAN YOU RELATE TO THIS?

The following is a case example illustrating some of the issues that can coexist with ADHD. Alice was a young, single elementary school teacher trying to fulfill her dream of publishing a children's book. However, Alice was unable to get much accomplished on her book beyond the title and was just barely able to keep up with the class she was teaching. The principal was upset by complaints from parents, and she had received an "unsatisfactory" on her most recent yearly evaluation. Alice was worried that she was going to be fired from her job.

Alice had done well in high school, although she reported always being disorganized and completing things at the last minute. She was very bright, took many honors and advanced placement courses, and worked hard to compensate for her lack of focus and difficulty paying attention. She had played on her high school soccer team and felt that the structure, discipline, and outdoor exercise had really helped her to do well overall. Her high school teachers and her mother (who was a college English professor) had been very supportive, and she received a great deal of help throughout high school in the form of individual attention, allowances for late work, and help organizing her time. Alice attended college in her hometown and continued to receive a great deal of support from her mother. She managed to graduate from college with a B average.

Alice reported that she had felt pressure from her mother to get a master's degree in education, and she didn't want to let her down after all her mother had done for her. After Alice barely made it through graduate school, the only school that offered her a job was in Florida, a long way from her home in New York. Alice was homesick from the time she began her job. She had difficulty adjusting to "small-town southern culture" and made few friends. She located a roommate through an online service but changed roommates every year because no one seemed to work out very well. Alice managed to "just get by" in her position, but she had to study all the time to keep up with the lesson planning. Her superiors frequently told her they thought she could do better, but she didn't see how she could do more. Alice reported that she really would have liked to have a boyfriend but didn't have the time and hadn't met anyone anyway. She found most of the single young men to be "immature, slobs, interested in one-night stands, or not interested in girls." Early in the school year, Alice had been told by the principal that she needed to prepare the kids for end-of-the-year state testing and follow strict guidelines. She wasn't sure of the consequences of not following the guidelines but had been afraid to ask, and she had avoided the principal most of the school year. Now, with a month left to go, she was panicking.

She had spent a great deal of time looking over the plans and had the children do some of the work here and there, but was not nearly as far as she should be with the tests looming in the next couple of weeks.

As the school year came to a close, Alice had become increasingly anxious. She felt she was letting her mother down, that she would be forced out of the school with nothing to show for the past 3 years, and that she was getting older and had no prospects of a serious relationship. She had quit working out at the gym, which made her feel even worse. The previous week she had lost her wallet, which held her license, apartment building key card, cash, and ATM card. Rather than go get a new license and call the credit card company, she had taken to her bed and stayed there for 2 days. Her current roommate finally told her "you look and smell like crap, you need to get counseling." She went to a local psychologist and was subsequently referred for a psychoeducational assessment.

Alice was evaluated for ADHD, with possible comorbid anxiety and depression. It was determined that she met the criteria for ADHD, predominantly inattentive type. She also met the criteria for diagnoses of depression and anxiety. Because she was quite bright and had good coping skills, Alice had managed to cope quite well up to the present time by working hard and getting support from her mother and teachers. However, as her job demands became more intense, she could not keep up. Her stress was compounded by not having a strong social support network, loneliness, dropping her normal exercise routine, and feeling that she was a disappointment to her mother. Her anxiety and depression seemed secondary to her ADHD, and her inattention and lack of focus left her unable to keep up with the complex demands of lesson planning, test prep, and teaching.

Alice was encouraged to disclose her diagnosis to the principal, and on the basis of her diagnosis of ADHD, she was entitled to receive accommodations under federal law. She met with the principal, who was understanding, and he agreed to meet with her twice each month to discuss her lesson plans. She signed up for ADHD coaching with a psychologist, which was offered at a local clinic, and worked with her coach to make a teaching schedule. Alice and her coach also decided that returning to a workout schedule at the gym would be helpful, so she signed up for a kick-boxing class in the hopes that it would provide good exercise and also help her to engage in a group (rather than solitary) routine. Alice's coach (a trained psychologist) also helped her to identify some of her negative cognitions (my mother won't love me if I fail, writing a book is impossible, I'll probably never get married or have children). She was able to replace these with more realistic thoughts and reported that this change in thinking reduced her anxiety tremendously. Alice also met with a psychiatrist at the clinic, who determined that the first-line treatment for ADHD (a stimulant) might not be suitable. Together, they decided that her depression was having a bigger negative impact on her life than was her anxiety; after meeting with her principal and her ADHD coach, she was feeling much less panicky and anxious. Therefore, the psychiatrist prescribed the nonstimulant-based Strattera (atomoxetine), which is a good choice for someone with ADHD and symptoms of depression. After about a week, Alice began to see a difference in her ability to concentrate, and she reported feeling much more positive overall.

This case shows just how complex ADHD can be. For some individuals, impairment will not be apparent until adulthood, and it may initially look like something else is the primary issue, such as anxiety or depression. Alice was similar to many young adults who did reasonably well throughout high school, college, and even graduate school. However, when you look closely at how hard they have worked compared with others, you usually find that a parent or teachers (often both) have helped them to structure their time and worked with them as tutors or mentors. Many people are quite surprised when they learn of a late onset diagnosis of ADHD, but they are often relieved because, in retrospect, it seems to explain many events and struggles in their lives. Often, it's the comorbid symptoms that really get the attention of referral sources. This case also shows how complex symptoms require a multimodal intervention. Any one of the interventions above would likely have been insufficient to get Alice back on track. But by attacking her difficulties from several directions, she was able to successfully move forward.

SUMMARY

Here are the important points you will want to take away from this chapter. Use the following checklist to note the areas you have thoroughly studied. Leave the box empty if it is an area you would like to come back to and review further.

☐ I understand the meaning and implications of the term *comorbidity*.

☐ I have learned how to recognize the common comorbidities that I need to watch out for.

☐ I have learned about the different types of anxiety.

☐ I have discovered new ways to practice a healthy lifestyle.

☐ I have learned new ways to reduce stress.

☐ I understand the symptoms of depression.

☐ I have tried some of the tips for helping depression.

☐ I understand how bipolar disorder is different from depression.

CHAPTER NINE

GETTING THE MOST
OUT OF MEDICATION

Never do today what you can put off until tomorrow.
—Matthew Browne

 Pharmacotherapy (taking medication) is a common treatment for ADHD in both children and adults. In this chapter, we first give you a brief overview of medications, along with a little bit of the history behind the use of prescription drugs. Next, we review the different types or classes of drugs that are commonly used to treat ADHD. You'll learn about the U.S. Food and Drug Administration (FDA) and why it's important. We go over both the positive benefits of taking drugs for ADHD, as well as some of the side effects. We explain some important safeguards when taking medications and give you a nontechnical explanation of how drugs work. We include a case study so that you can see how taking drugs can be effectively managed. Finally, we've created two tables (9.1 and 9.2) that summarize the important FDA and drug

Table 9.1 FDA Approved Drugs for ADHD Treatment	
Brand name	**Generic name**
	Stimulants
Adderall	Amphetamine and dextroamphetamine combined (mixed amphetamine salts)
Concerta	Methylphenidate
Daytrana	Methylphenidate
Desoxyn	Methamphetamine
Dexedrine	Dextroamphetamine
Focalin	Dexmethylphenidate
Metadate	Methylphenidate
Methylin	Methylphenidate
Ritalin	Methylphenidate
Vyvanse	Lisdexamfetamine
	Non-stimulant (selective norepinephrine reuptake inhibitor)
Strattera	Atomoxetine

Table 9.2 Additional Antidepressants	
Brand name	**Generic name**
Aventyl	Nortriptyline (tricyclic antidepressant)
Cymbalta	Duloxetine (selective serotonin and norepinephrine reuptake inhibitor)
Effexor	Venlafaxine (serotonin-norepinephrine reuptake inhibitor)
Nardil	Phenelzine (monoamine oxidase inhibitor)
Norpramin	Desipramine (tricyclic antidepressant)
Pamelor	Nortriptyline (tricyclic antidepressant)
Parnate	Tranylcypromine (monomine oxidase inhibitor)
Tofranil	Imipranine (tricyclic antidepressant)
Wellbutrin	Bupropion

manufacturer information you need to know for some of the most commonly used drugs.

WHAT THE EXPERTS SAY

The National Institute of Mental Health has estimated that approximately 50% of children who need medication for ADHD still need it as adults. Remember the core symptoms of ADHD? They are difficulty paying attention, high activity, and impulsivity. These general symptoms can usually be reduced with medication, especially in the short term. It's estimated that about 70% of children and adolescents who take stimulant medication will show significant improvement. The exact percentage is not yet known for adults, although reports have indicated that it is somewhat less than the effectiveness rates for children.

Those adults who do not show improvement in their ADHD symptoms using drugs are called *nonresponders*. A nonresponder is defined as someone whose core symptoms do not decrease by at least half or who have such serious side effects that they can't tolerate the drug. But, as you will read later, there are many options for you if you happen to be a nonresponder or choose not to take medication.

Hundreds of studies have reported on the effectiveness of medications in children and adolescents with ADHD, but not nearly so many studies in adults. However, there are studies with adults that have shown benefits in alertness, short-term memory, visual memory, and spatial planning. Those adults who do respond well to medication have reported that they are less fidgety and restless, they can focus better, their attention span improves, things seem more

233

clear, they do not interrupt others as much, and/or they are better at finishing tasks.

However, drugs are not a panacea; they won't magically make you a different person, nor will they undo years of ingrained behavior that you have learned. They won't change your IQ. They won't necessarily improve your social skills, organizational abilities, time management skills, and self-confidence. One fairly large study of adults on medication found that almost all of the participants continued to have problems at work, even after taking medication. The second most common area that was not improved by drugs was interpersonal relationships. Many adults continue to struggle in their interactions with their spouse, children, relatives, or friends. That doesn't mean that these areas won't improve, only that they won't improve immediately just because you take medication.

On the positive side, it is believed that medications give people with ADHD the ability to focus and attend, so that they can more easily work on changing these areas of their lives. A good metaphor for this is trying to read a book by candlelight. Candlelight can be very dim, and you may have difficulty seeing the small print reading by it. Taking medication might be compared with turning on a 100-watt lightbulb. All of a sudden you have the ability to see clearly. The lightbulb won't make you a good reader or define words that you don't know; you have to do that yourself. But it will give you an environment that lets you read more easily.

So what's the bottom line? If you are an adult, medication alone is probably not going to alleviate all the symptoms and learned behaviors that you have developed over the years as a result of ADHD. We strongly recommend that if you choose to use medication, you combine drugs with some other form of intervention, such as cognitive–behavioral therapy or ADHD coaching. See Chapter 10 for a discussion of good treatments to go along with pharmacotherapy.

TYPES OF ADHD MEDICATION

Stimulants

The original treatment of choice for ADHD, amphetamine, was identified as early as the 1930s. Since that time, amphetamine has been repeatedly shown to produce a significant improvement in all three symptom areas and works well regardless of your diagnostic subtype (primarily inattentive, primarily hyperactive-impulsive, or combined type). Thus, amphetamines remained the primary treatment for over 50 years.

In 1968, another stimulant, methylphenidate (widely known as Ritalin) was approved by the U.S. Food and Drug Administration, and it has since replaced amphetamines as the drug of choice. Technically, amphetamine and methylphenidate refer to two different molecules, both of which are stimulants, and most of the trade names you have probably heard of are just variants of one of these two molecules. Today, stimulants continue to be the most commonly used class of drugs for the treatment of ADHD. Trade names that you might be familiar with include Adderall, Concerta, Desoxyn, Dexedrine, Dextrostat, Focalin, Metadate, and Methylin. Because the two molecules have different effects on the body, some individuals tolerate and respond better to amphetamine(s), and others respond better to methylphenidate; however, if neither of the stimulants is effective, there are other classes of drugs that can be useful.

Medications used to treat ADHD:

- Stimulants
- Nonstimulants
- Antidepressants
- Blood pressure medication
- Seizure medication
- Sleep medication
- Antipsychotic medication

Antidepressants

The second most popular class of drugs, after the stimulants, are the antidepressants. Dr. Thomas Spencer, who is affiliated with both Massachusetts General Hospital and Harvard Medical School, has written extensively about antidepressant medications for ADHD. He summarized four types commonly used: tricylics, bupropion, monoamine oxidase inhibitors (MAOIs), and both selective and specific reuptake inhibitors (SSRIs and SNRIs). According to Dr. Spencer, tricyclics are beneficial because they are longer lasting, they do not have a high abuse potential, and they tend not to cause insomnia. They can be especially useful for someone who has symptoms of anxiety and depression along with ADHD symptoms. Bupropion is a nonstimulant antidepressant commonly used to treat major depression. MAOIs are used less frequently in the treatment of ADHD, and there is some evidence that they can negatively interact with food (such as cheese). There is also concern that they should not be used in combination with stimulants. The SSRIs and SNRIs are undergoing more widespread research trials, and further study is needed. Strattera (in the class atomoxetine, which is one type of SNRI) is currently the only antidepressant approved by the FDA for adult use as an ADHD drug. (Intuniv is approved for ADHD treatment in children ages 6 to 17.)

You may have heard of the following brand names of anti-depressants: Aventyl, Cymbalta, Effexor, Nardil, Norpramin, Parnate, Pamelor, Strattera, Tofranil, and Wellbutrin. Antidepressants are generally thought to be better for treating mild to moderate ADHD. They become effective in 2 to 3 days, but it can be 8 to 10 weeks before full benefits are seen. The rate of nonresponders is thought to be higher for the antidepressants than for the stimulants. Also, antidepressants sometimes lose their effectiveness after a year or two. Antidepressants might be a particularly good choice if you have symptoms of depression or anxiety along with your symptoms of ADHD. In many cases, antidepressants are prescribed in conjunction with a stimulant; however, this should be done very carefully on the advice of your doctor, as some stimulants and antidepressants (particularly MAOIs) should not be combined.

Less Common Medications

Drugs other than stimulants or antidepressants might be considered if you are a nonresponder to those medications; if you have serious side effects; if you have a history of drug abuse; if you develop a tolerance to your current prescription medication; or if you have a worrisome history of heart problems, bipolar disorder, schizophrenia, or other disorders. Drugs that have been approved for sleep disorders, high blood pressure, thought disorders, and seizures, although not approved by the FDA for ADHD, have been used for ADHD and found to be effective for some individuals. Some drugs that you might have heard of are Provigil (normally used for sleep disorders), Risperdal (normally used for schizophrenia or bipolar disorder), Intuniv (normally used for high blood pressure), and Tegretol (normally used to control seizures).

Remember These Facts About Medication

For many of the ADHD medications, you will have the choice of a short-acting, an intermediate-acting, and a long-acting form of the drug. The short-acting forms of the drug are usually taken two or three times a day and the long-acting ones just once a day. For those who can't remember to take their drugs, or if your work or school day makes it difficult to take drugs during the day, the long-acting drugs can be a good choice. These are called *extended release,* (usually indicated by an XR after the name) and their effects usually last 8 to 12 hours. The immediate-release drugs often need to be taken every 3 to 5 hours but have the benefit of quick effects that can be targeted to specific situations (such as studying for an exam or attending a meeting).

Understanding FDA Approval and Drugs Your Doctor Might Prescribe

The U.S. Food and Drug Administration (FDA) approves drugs for ADHD. However, most of the drugs that have been approved have been for children and adolescents, not for adults. The only ADHD drugs approved by the FDA for adults (as of June 2010) are Vyvanse (a stimulant), Adderall XR (a stimulant), and Strattera (an antidepressant). Just because an ADHD drug hasn't been approved by the FDA for adults doesn't mean that you can't take it. A physician can legally prescribe a drug *off-label.* That means

Understanding FDA Approval and Drugs Your Doctor Might Prescribe (*Continued*)

he can write you a prescription and you can take that drug. However, it is illegal for the drug manufacturer to advertise or in any way promote a drug for a specific use that has not been approved by the FDA. For example, Effexor has been approved by the FDA as an antidepressant. Therefore, the company that makes Effexor can only advertise it as an antidepressant. However, your doctor can legally prescribe it for you as a treatment for ADHD. Generally, physicians only do this when there are scientific studies showing that the drug works for ADHD. It can take many years to get FDA approval, so it commonly happens that the evidence for a drug exists a long time before the FDA actually approves it.

WHY MEDICATIONS WORK

Scientists don't know the exact reason why ADHD medications work. It is suspected that ADHD can be caused by both genetic factors and by certain predisposing environmental events (such as low birth weight, maternal smoking during pregnancy, or prenatal exposure to toxins). Both genetics and prenatal environment seem to cause difficulties in the way the brain works.

Neurotransmitters are chemicals that help the different parts of the brain communicate. These chemicals don't seem to be released correctly in someone with ADHD. Neurotransmitters thought to be important in ADHD are epinephrine, norepinephrine, dopamine, and serotonin. Drugs such as stimulants and antidepressants regulate impulsive behavior and improve attention span and focus by regulating the levels of these chemicals, which help transmit signals between nerves.

The stimulants increase the ability of the brain to be vigilant, to focus, and to inhibit unwanted behaviors. This is why the behavior of stimulants is commonly referred to as *paradoxical,* or opposite to what you would expect. Normal people take stimulants to increase activity level, so it is described as paradoxical that a stimulant decreases activity level in someone with ADHD. What's really happening, though, is that the stimulant is stimulating or increasing your ability to focus, self-regulate, and inhibit your behaviors, which looks to outside observers as if you are decreasing your inattentiveness, impulsivity, and hyperactivity.

As you might guess, it's difficult to know exactly what's going on in your brain unless you can actually open it up and examine it. So scientists have to rely on noninvasive procedures that, fortunately, are becoming much more sophisticated. These techniques usually include some sort of neuroimaging procedure. Newer research has suggested that the two types of stimulants, amphetamines and methylphenidate, work a bit differently with regard to the way they release and block the transmission of dopamine and norepinephrine. They also work differently with regard to the way they metabolize in the body. This is why it is suggested that if you are a nonresponder to one of these drug types, you should try the other one. The following is a list of things that you should mention to your doctor before starting or changing your medication regimen.

Medication Alert

Be sure to tell your physician any of the following:
1. If you are nursing, pregnant, or plan to become pregnant.
2. If you are taking any other medications, either prescription or over-the-counter.
3. If you have a history of any medical problems, particularly high blood pressure, seizures, heart disease, glaucoma, or liver or kidney disease.
4. If you have a history of drug or alcohol problems.
5. If you have ever had problems with depression, bipolar disorder, anxiety, or thought disorders.
6. If you become agitated or irritable, or develop suicidal thoughts.
7. If you develop irregular heartbeats or fainting spells.

COMMON SIDE EFFECTS OF MEDICATIONS

The good news is that medications are very effective for many adults in reducing the symptoms of ADHD. The bad news is that many people experience some level of side effects. Because these side effects tend to be similar for drugs in the same class, we have summarized them by class. However, keep in mind that your particular drug (or response to a drug) might be different, and you should read the medication guide carefully.

Stimulants

Loss of appetite, dry mouth, insomnia, nausea, and headaches are all common side effects of ADHD stimulant medications. A rise in blood pressure can also occur as a result of a stimulant medication. Often, the effects are mild and last only a few weeks, but this is not always the case. One key to minimizing side effects is to make sure you are on the optimal dose of the medication. There is a delicate balance between getting enough of the drug to alleviate your symptoms and not getting so much that your side effects are unmanageable. Signs of exceeding an optimal dose are similar to having too much caffeine: mild depression, jitters, literally feeling your heart beating, headache, irritability, hand tremor, and loss of appetite. Some individuals have noticed that when they take too much of a stimulant they have a reverse effect, popularly described as the "zombie syndrome." They feel slow and lethargic, as if their thoughts and feelings have been slowed down. This has sometimes been reported, even with the correct dosage, during the first day or two that the drug is started.

Another term you will want to remember is the *dosing rebound*. This can be a bit confusing, because the same symptoms have been linked to two very different causes. In the first instance, you have probably taken too high a dose and feel the typical high-dose side effects just described. In the second instance, you have the same side effects but only when the medicine is wearing off; in this case, the cause can be a dosing rebound. This means the level of medication in your blood is dropping too quickly, which causes you to crash. You can work with your doctor to prevent dosing rebound by taking a very small dose of the immediate-release version of the same medication shortly before the time of day when rebound occurs, smoothing out the effects so the drop-off is more gradual. Again, be sure to consult your doctor and try this only under his or her guidance.

Zombie syndrome: A common side effect of stimulants wherein the user feels slow and lethargic.

There have been concerns that taking stimulants can lead to abuse and that they can become addictive. Research by several leaders in the field has suggested that the use of stimulants does not lead to substance abuse or dependence. In fact, a group of researchers led by Dr. Timothy Wilens of Harvard Medical School found that teens with ADHD who took stimulant medications were less likely to abuse drugs than those who did not take stimulant medications. Stimulants could be a concern primarily for someone who is already abusing drugs. Someone who currently has a history of drug abuse should probably not take a stimulant medication for ADHD.

Antidepressants

Antidepressants can also have side effects. The most common ones seem to be loss of appetite, upset stomach, nausea, headache, dizziness, mood swings, and tiredness or sleepiness. The drug Strattera (atomoxetine) includes an FDA-required warning that it has been associated with suicidal thoughts in children and adolescents. However, according to the FDA, studies with adults have shown no risk of suicidal ideation in adults who take Strattera.

Several websites offer advice on how to deal with common side effects. One of those (http://www.webmd.com) lists the following suggestions. Many of these suggestions have been tried primarily in children and adolescents; however, you may still find them helpful.

- *Stomach upset:* Take your medication with food. Eat healthy snacks during the day. If you can take your dose a little later in the morning, this could decrease chances of stomach upset.

- *Headaches:* Take your medication with food; without food, the medication is absorbed more quickly, which causes blood levels of the medication to rise, which can lead to headaches. Try switching to a long-acting medication; sometimes headaches can be due to the rebound effect when your short-acting medication is wearing off.
- *Sleep difficulties:* Try to maintain a consistent time to go to sleep and wake up. Develop bedtime rituals. Avoid caffeinated beverages in the afternoon or evening. Dedicate the bedroom to sleep only, not to work or entertainment. Use relaxation techniques at bedtime.
- *Dizziness:* This often results from a medication dosage that is too high. Check your blood pressure and consult your physician if it's higher than normal.

Medication Alert—Serious Side Effects

In 2007, the U.S. Food and Drug Administration (FDA) began requiring all manufacturers of ADHD drugs to develop patient guidelines that warn consumers about possible cardiovascular risks, as well as risks of possible psychiatric side effects. All patients must be given these guidelines any time they receive their ADHD medication. The FDA cautioned that there have been reports of sudden death in patients with underlying serious heart problems or defects and reports of stroke and heart attack in adults with certain risk factors. The FDA also warned that ADHD medicines revealed a slight increased risk (about 1 per 1,000) for psychiatric adverse events, such as hearing voices, becoming suspicious for no reason, or becoming manic, even in patients who did not have previous psychiatric

Medication Alert—Serious Side Effects *(Continued)*

problems. The ADHD drugs that are included in this warning are only those drugs that are approved by the FDA for the treatment of ADHD. The only drugs approved by the FDA for the treatment of ADHD are stimulants, as well as the nonstimulant atomoxetine.

HOW TO MAKE YOUR MEDICATION WORK FOR YOU

Some sources estimate that up to half of adults who start a medication stop taking it after 4 to 6 months. They may be frustrated with the side effects or they may feel that the benefits are just not worth the side effects. It's vitally important that you work with your doctor to find the right drug and the right dose so that you can benefit from pharmacotherapy. Studies have shown that the way a stimulant works for you is not consistently related to age, weight, or symptom severity. Rather, it depends on your individual body chemistry, which is genetically determined. Individuals absorb different amounts of stimulants into their bloodstream, and the amount can vary widely. That's why you should start with a low dose and then carefully increase it under your doctor's supervision to find out what works best for you. You may take the same dose as your friend who weighs the same as you, but you may absorb twice as much of it. Individuals also have different rates of metabolism. That means that after you absorb the drug into your bloodstream, you metabolize it through your liver and kidneys and out through your urine. The rate at which you metabolize the drug determines how long it has an effect on your symptoms.

Many experts recommend that if you have no other conditions to deal with (such as depression, anxiety, drug dependence, bipolar disorder), you should always start with a stimulant, because stimulants tend to have the best results. Try both an amphetamine and a methylphenidate (both are stimulants) if one or the other doesn't work. If stimulants are not effective for you, then you should consider an antidepressant and, finally, one of the drugs commonly used for other disorders (sleep disorders, high blood pressure, thought disorders, and seizures).

Alternatively, if you have symptoms of depression, you might want to start with an antidepressant. Antidepressants seem to be different from stimulants in that the proper dose is based more on weight than on body chemistry. A benefit of the nonstimulant medications is that they are not a controlled substance, and so they can be used more safely by someone who has an ongoing substance abuse problem. They also tend not to cause insomnia, which can be common with stimulants.

The first weeks and months of taking a new drug are critical. You need to carefully monitor your side effects. Keep a daily journal if possible, so that when you meet with your doctor you can give a detailed report of your eating habits, sleep, side effects, and benefits. Keep track of how the drug works during different activities (such as work, exercise, relaxing, or reading).

It is also very important to work with your doctor to determine if you have conditions other than ADHD that may interfere with your ADHD medication. Many adults with ADHD will have at least one other mental health disorder during their lifetime. These other disorders include anxiety disorders, depressive disorders, bipolar disorder, and substance use disorders. Be sure to read Chapter 8 if you think you have one of these other disorders. If this is the case, then you may need to work with your doctor to adjust your medication to make certain that you are controlling all of your symptoms. You may need to decide which condition is most distressing to your overall quality of life and treat that one first. Sometimes the medication for your other disorder can help your ADHD symptoms; unfortunately, sometimes that medication can make your ADHD symptoms worse. You will need to work with your doctor to select a drug or combination of drugs to manage your particular symptoms.

Medication Alert—Drug Interactions

If you are taking a stimulant medication for ADHD, check with your physician before taking any medications for colds or allergies. Common over-the-counter decongestants such as Sudafed contain pseudoephedrine, which can increase the side effects of your ADHD stimulant medication, perhaps causing increased heart or pulse rate. You might want to consider using a nasal spray rather than a decongestant, skipping your ADHD medication temporarily, or making sure that your cold medicine does not contain pseudoephedrine.

CAN YOU RELATE TO THIS?

Mike was a junior in college, majoring in business. He aspired to work with his father one day in his father's real estate office; however, he was beginning to despair of this happening. Mike's father had insisted that he obtain his college degree, and Mike was barely maintaining a 2.0 average. He sought help at the university mental health clinic on the advice of his advisor and was evaluated and diagnosed with ADHD, combined type.

During his evaluation, Mike related that he had experienced difficulty in school for as long as he could remember but managed to get by with help from his parents and teachers. He reported that his difficulties "skyrocketed" when he left home to attend college. He lost his student ID six times during his freshman year and accumulated more than a dozen parking tickets. He had tried working part time but was fired from three different "menial" jobs as a waiter for poor performance. Mike had pledged a fraternity his freshman year and was devastated when he was kicked out the fall of his junior year. He claimed to have no idea why he was kicked out, saying that the official reason—missed meetings—could not have been the real reason. Mike seemed to have little insight into his difficulties. He had failed or withdrawn from several courses, primarily for missing too many classes or not being able to keep up with assignments. He reported partying and drinking more than he knew was good for him and feeling that his life was "totally out of control."

After his evaluation and diagnosis, Mike scheduled an appointment with the psychiatrist at the student counseling center on campus. He also continued to meet weekly with a counselor. The psychiatrist initially started Mike with 20 mg, twice per day, of immediate-release Adderall. Mike soon reported a significant loss of appetite. He stated that he would go all day and "totally forget to eat." After losing 10 pounds, he began setting his phone alarm twice a day to remind him to eat. He also left notes for himself at home to remind himself to take a snack with him to classes. Mike also noted difficulty sleeping, saying that his body was exhausted but his mind just kept going and going. The more he tried to will himself to sleep, the more frustrated he got, which resulted in hours of lying awake. By the time he finally fell asleep, he would be so exhausted that he would often sleep through his alarm clock in the morning, missing class as a result. Then he would take his initial dose of medication too late, which often contributed to another sleepless night.

Mike also described "crashes" that occurred as the drug was wearing off. He would feel depressed, irritable, and tired and would often take an additional dose of the drug when he felt a crash coming on. The crashes were so aversive that Mike would overmedicate regardless of the time of day or consequences of the extra dose. Mike was extremely discouraged at the end of his first month on Adderall but continued to work with both his counselor and psychiatrist. After 3 months of careful experimentation, Mike found that his best regimen consisted of 30 mg of extended-release Adderall once in the morning, followed by 10 mg of immediate-release Adderall in the afternoon.

After finding the best dosage of his medication, Mike reported that "my life changed forever; I feel like I have a future." He was grateful that he had stuck it out and worked with his doctor and counselor because he had felt several times like giving up. Mike was excited to report that he was passing all his courses with at least a *B* average and that he had already been promised a summer job working with his father, which was "my ultimate reward, to have my father proud of me." He reported that he was able to focus, finish tasks, and actually think through the consequences of his actions. He had not had a parking ticket in 3 months, partly because he was riding his bike more, which had the added benefit of helping him stay in shape. Mike lamented that "it breaks my heart to think there are people out there like me, trapped in the prison of ADHD. I'm really glad I had a great team who worked with me to turn things around."

It should be clear from this case study that it is extremely important that you work with your doctor and/or clinician to make sure that you are on the best medication for you and at the best dosage for you. Remember, everyone is different, and there is no way to know how your body will react. You may benefit from a stimulant, an antidepressant, or even a drug normally used for high blood pressure or sleep disorders. The key is to keep your spirits up, realize up front that you will probably need to make adjustments before you find the best drug for you, and know that it will very likely pay off with positive results in the end.

A QUICK GUIDE TO MEDICATIONS

Don't despair if this chapter seems a bit overwhelming. There are many drugs available for ADHD, and it's difficult to keep them straight. Keep in mind that your doctor is the expert, and you don't have to know all the facts. (Just make sure your doctor has experience in treating patients with ADHD.) It can be especially daunting to read the medication guide that comes with your ADHD drug. The FDA recently standardized and shortened these guides and provides a handy website where you can easily review the drug you might be considering. Keep in mind that you can find a lot of information on the Internet; if you put in the name of a drug, you are likely to get thousands of hits, and there is no way to know whether what you are reading is accurate. The medication guides put out by the FDA have all been carefully scrutinized and approved by the FDA, so you can be sure they are accurate. Each guide will have the following information:

- Problems associated with the drug
- Precautions, such as when and what to tell your doctor
- How to take the drug (dosage, can you chew or crush it)
- Side effects
- Who should not take the drug
- Whether the drug can be taken with other medicines
- How to store the drug
- Ingredients in the drug

The drugs in Table 9.1 (p. 232) are all FDA approved for the treatment of adult ADHD, and information on them can be found at http://www.fda.gov/Drugs/DrugSafety/ucm085729.htm. The antidepressants in Table 9.2 (p. 232) are not FDA approved for adult ADHD but are commonly prescribed off-label.

SUMMARY

Here are the important points you will want to take away from this chapter. Use the following checklist to note the areas you have thoroughly studied. Leave the box empty if it is an area you would like to come back to and review further.

☐ I understand ways to tell if I am a nonresponder to medication.

☐ I understand that medication might help some but not all ADHD symptoms.

☐ I have considered using medication in combination with a psychological intervention.

☐ I have learned about the most common types of ADHD medications and the way they work.

☐ I understand that many medications produce unwanted side effects.

☐ I have learned how to make my medications work for me.

☐ I have checked the FDA guidelines for my medication.

CHAPTER TEN

FINDING THE RIGHT COUNSELOR, COACH, OR OTHER TREATMENT SOLUTION

You should try therapy. It's like a really easy game show where the correct answer to every question is "Because of my mother".
—Robin Greenspan

 If you've gone to a parent, teacher, friend, professional organizer, or mental health professional who did not specialize in ADHD for help with your day-to-day functioning, chances are good that their efforts did not help you much, as these individuals may have an incomplete or incorrect understanding of ADHD. You may feel disillusioned and demoralized and have learned to expect disappointment as a natural consequence of your efforts. This unfortunate and sometimes devastating mind-set can be altered. If ADHD is properly managed, you can have significant and sometimes dramatic improvements in life functioning.

253

Sometimes simply being diagnosed and treated by a professional who really understands ADHD can bring tremendous relief to individuals with ADHD. You may remember that when you were diagnosed and you received an explanation for your lifelong pattern of difficulties, you finally felt understood for the first time. Just the realization that somebody truly understands and empathizes with the issues that you have been struggling with can be extraordinarily therapeutic. The challenge then becomes devising a treatment plan to help you live more effectively and ultimately gain better control over your ADHD-related behaviors.

In this chapter, we outline some of the current nonmedication-based treatment interventions for adults with ADHD, including the following:

- counseling/therapy,
- exercise and nutrition,
- ADHD coaching,
- accommodations, and
- multimodal treatment.

In addition, we provide a case example of a young man who tried unsuccessfully to treat his ADHD before finding the right service for him, a quiz to help you figure out which treatment option may be right for you, tips on locating an ADHD specialist, questions to ask a specialist, and help with overcoming any fears of treatment that you might have.

Adults living with ADHD have several treatment options that can help them to lead a more happy and productive life. Although nonmedication-based treatments do not "cure" ADHD, they can certainly help you cope with the emotional, attitudinal, and behavioral issues as well as the co-occurring conditions often associated with ADHD, such as depression and anxiety. Still, no one intervention technique has proven effective for all individuals with the disorder. As the consumer, it is up to you to research and attempt the treatment or combination of treatments that feel right for you.

WHAT THE EXPERTS SAY

At this time, psychopharmacology (discussed at length in Chapter 9 on medication) is the only rigorously studied treatment option for adults with ADHD. However, in controlled studies of stimulants and open studies of other medications commonly used to treat ADHD, 20% to 50% of adults are considered *nonresponders*. This means that the medications do not reduce symptoms sufficiently or the person suffers from bad side effects. Moreover, adults who are considered *responders* typically show a reduction in only 50% or fewer of the core symptoms of ADHD. Given these data, medication alone is not considered the best treatment method for adults with ADHD.

Although medication may improve many of the central symptoms of ADHD (attentional problems, high activity, impulsivity), most experts agree that it does not provide a person with concrete strategies and skills for coping with the disorder. Imagine a time when you sustained a physical injury. You probably took a pain-relieving medication to temporarily mask the soreness. Meanwhile, you knew that the medication did not actually help to heal the injury—to do that, you needed to nurse it and exercise and mobilize it until it was again functioning to your standards. Similarly, quality of life impairments such as underachievement, disorganization, and problems with time management; weekly work or school-related tasks; and relationship difficulties associated with ADHD in adulthood require active problem solving. These things can be achieved with skills training over and above medication management. To prove this point, the National Institute of Mental Health conducted a Multimodal Treatment of ADHD Study in 1997.[1] This was the largest randomized treatment study ever done, and the outcome solidified the fact that psychosocial treatments such as counseling or coaching, in combination with medication, result in the best outcomes for individuals with ADHD.

CAN YOU RELATE TO THIS?

The following case describes a man who sought treatment for issues related to depression and ADHD symptoms, including lack of organization and time management, relationship problems, and trouble focusing. Eric was diagnosed with ADHD by his family doctor in the late 1990s during his sophomore year of high school. He was prescribed Ritalin and took it on and off through college. Despite taking medication, he continued to struggle with poor grades and did not attempt any other form of treatment. He also had several undesirable side effects from the medication, including trouble

---

[1]The MTA Cooperative Group. (1997). NIMH collaborative multimodal treatment study of children with ADHD (MTA): Design, methodology, and protocol evolution. *Journal of Attention Disorders, 2,* 141–158.

sleeping, which made his ADHD symptoms worse. During college Eric had to drop and repeat several credits, and he finally managed to barely graduate with a low grade-point average after 5½ years. This self-described "failure," along with a failed relationship with his serious college girlfriend, caused Eric to spiral into a depression.

After college, Eric moved home for several months and applied for a number of jobs without success. He let his laundry pile up, left dirty dishes all over the house, and rarely left his bedroom. Finally, his mom insisted that he see a therapist if he wanted to continue to live at home. They found a counselor nearby who was covered by their insurance (although he was not an expert on ADHD) and made an appointment. Eric found the therapist likeable and enjoyed talking to him but felt that the "generic talk therapy" wasn't getting him anywhere with his ADHD symptoms. Eric stated that their conversations centered mostly on his disappointments and feelings of depression. His impression was that even though the therapist knew Eric had an ADHD diagnosis, because his issues didn't center on school or work and the therapist did not specialize in ADHD, he did not give it much attention. Eric further said that although he always felt "a little better" immediately following their sessions, he felt like this was temporary and that therapy wasn't helping him to "get any further in life."

After almost a year, Eric decided to terminate therapy. He landed a part-time job as an executive assistant for a small business and was able to save up enough money to move out of his parents' home. For awhile his depression seemed to lift enough to satisfy him. He even started dating a new woman, and things were going pretty well. However, now 25, Eric found himself pressured by his girlfriend to get engaged, and his boss was beginning to require more from him at work. Eric was beginning to spiral into another depression. Although he loved his girlfriend, something in him could not make the commitment, and he was having a hard time staying organized and focused in the office.

Because Eric had tried both medication and therapy and felt that neither had really helped, he struggled with what to do. Fortunately, he spoke to a friend, who let him know of a counselor and coach nearby who specialized in ADHD. As the new counselor and Eric talked, it became clear to him that he was a good candidate for ADHD coaching and cognitive–behavioral therapy (CBT) and that the reasons why his prior treatments had not worked well could be easily explained. When it came to his initial diagnosis, Eric's doctor had done little in terms of explaining the ADHD diagnosis or treatment options. This left Eric and his family to make their own assumptions about what ADHD was, and the doctor's prescription for stimulants led them to believe that medication was the only and best way to treat the disorder. Once on the medication, Eric did not communicate his struggles with side effects to his doctor and did not ask about alternative treatment options. In terms of therapy, the original counselor that Eric saw did not specialize in ADHD and unknowingly undermined Eric's rehabilitation by placing little value on this diagnosis. Likewise, this therapist was not specifically trained in CBT, and Eric did not realize that psychological counseling had many different approaches. As a result of these experiences, Eric naturally came to assume that neither medication nor therapy was the right answer.

The specialist was able to convince Eric to give ADHD coaching and counseling a shot. Eric started having weekly sessions, engaging in both coaching and cognitive–behavioral methods. By setting some realistic goals and working with his counselor to reach those goals, Eric became more comfortable and effective at work, earning him a promotion; was able to put his fears aside and propose to his girlfriend; and best of all, started to "feel good about life again." Today, Eric is happily married with a baby on the way and working at a job he enjoys.

The case of Eric demonstrates several issues common to adults with ADHD when seeking treatment. Many individuals tend to become disillusioned and disappointed by their first attempts to seek services simply because they don't know what to look for or the right questions to ask. However, the right treatment, with or without the use of prescription medication, can help most adults with ADHD begin to reduce their symptoms and increase their arsenal of coping mechanisms. The following are descriptions of the current popular nonmedication-based treatment methods you may want to consider.

 COUNSELING

Individual counseling and counseling groups can provide information, advocacy, instruction, and support. Some types of therapy or therapeutic interventions that have been suggested for adults with ADHD are

- CBT,
- social skills training,
- group therapy, and
- mindfulness meditation.

Cognitive–Behavioral Therapy

CBT has been shown to be one of the best forms of counseling for adults with ADHD. The use of CBT with those diagnosed with ADHD is powerfully backed by evidence. CBT is a form of psychotherapy that focuses on changing maladaptive patterns of thinking and the underlying beliefs that guide such thoughts. The hope is that learning to change these distorted thoughts can then lead to changes in behavior. For example, an adult with ADHD might think, "I am lazy." A cognitive–behavioral therapist would challenge this person to test this hypothesis and prove it wrong. Ideally, once the individual gains evidence that he or she is not actually lazy, his or her sense of self-worth and self-esteem increase, and fear-based behavior diminishes.

The ABC model of CBT consists of three parts to describe how you arrive at conclusions and whether these are healthy and productive. Understanding it is as simple as "ABC":

- *Activating event*—the actual event and your immediate interpretations of the event
- *Beliefs* about the event—this evaluation can be rational or irrational
- *Consequences*—how you feel and what you do or other thoughts

Next, we present two scenarios, each consisting of the same activating event. However, as you can see, your evaluation and belief about the event can drastically change your outlook and improve your functioning as an adult with ADHD.

Scenario 1

   A. Susan receives a poor performance review from her boss that states she seems "unmotivated, sloppy, and unfocused."

   B. Susan thinks, "I am such a stupid, lazy idiot."

   C. Susan stops giving any effort at her job and eventually gets laid off.

Scenario 2

   A. Susan receives a poor performance review from her boss that states she seems "unmotivated, sloppy, and unfocused."

   B. Susan thinks, "I could really use some support to tackle my issues with organization, procrastination, and paying attention."

   C. Susan begins ADHD coaching sessions, develops strategies to overcome her weaknesses at work, and earns a promotion.

The key to understanding CBT is realizing that your moods and actions are driven by what you tell yourself in each situation and are not a direct result of the circumstances in your life. A therapist who specializes in CBT can help you to change your thought patterns using several techniques, such as journaling, relaxation, positive affirmations, and reflection.

Social Skills Training

Research has demonstrated that skill-building approaches, such as social skills training, have not been of much benefit to adults with

ADHD. Social skills training is designed to help the individual learn appropriate behaviors and behave in a more socially acceptable way. In terms of ADHD, such behaviors may include impulsivity, aggression, and anger. Sessions are usually held in small-group settings so that members can practice and role play with one another for a designated amount of time. Such groups seem to have more effect on children with the disorder than on adults. Additionally, the short-term psychosocial treatment effects that do take place often do not typically generalize outside the context in which they are applied.

Group Therapy

Although group therapy is underutilized and underresearched, hearing how others cope and manage their symptoms, realizing there are others who have similar problems, and having a safe and supportive place to ask questions and try out new behaviors and interpersonal skills are all valuable advantages of group counseling. On the other hand, groups reduce the amount of personal attention an individual will receive. Unless the therapist leading the group is mindful of each participant, it is easy for talkative types and attention seekers to take up much of the group's time and energy. Plus, suggestions made by other members may or may not be agreeable to the advice of a professional. Still, for those looking for a budget-friendly, supportive environment to help manage their ADHD symptoms, group therapy can be a great option.

MINDFULNESS MEDITATION

A cost-effective option that many professionals in the field argue is helpful in improving focus and attention as well as reducing stress for adults with ADHD is the practice of mindfulness meditation. Doctors at the University of California–Los Angeles have begun to examine the effectiveness of mindfulness meditation for adults with ADHD, with promising results. According to the authors,[2]

> Mindfulness meditation involves experiential learning via silent periods of sitting meditation or slow walking and purposeful attention to daily activities. Relaxation, although often induced during the training, is not the sole goal of the activity; rather, the main activity is a cognitive and intention-based process characterized by self-regulation and attention to the present moment with an open and accepting orientation towards one's experiences.

Mindfulness meditation can be broken down into three basic steps: (a) bringing attention to an "attentional anchor," such as breathing; (b) noting that distraction occurred and letting go of the distraction; and (c) refocusing back to the "attentional anchor." Research has demonstrated that mindfulness meditation can reduce self-reported ADHD symptoms, improve attentional task performance, modulate EEG patterns, alter dopamine levels, and change neural activity.

---

[2]Zylowska, L., Ackerman, D., Yang, M., Futrell, J., Horton, N., Hale, T., Pataki, C., & Smalley, S. (2007). Mindfulness meditation training in adults and adolescents with ADHD. *Journal of Attention Disorders, 11,* 737–746. doi: 10.1177/1087054707308502

Neurofeedback

Neurofeedback is a highly controversial technique that involves teaching an individual to produce more focused brain wave patterns and was created to reduce ADHD symptoms such as distractibility and impulsivity. Using computer software to display scenes on which the user is supposed to focus, electrodes are attached to the scalp to measure the brain's electrical activity. Although there is some evidence of its effectiveness, many professionals feel that neurofeedback is simply a more costly version of mindfulness meditation.

EXERCISE AND NUTRITION

Want a cheap and proven way to change your brain without the risk of side effects? Try exercise. Although keeping fit is important to all people, it can be particularly beneficial to adults with ADHD.

John Ratey, MD, an associate clinical professor of psychiatry at Harvard Medical School and author of *Spark: The Revolutionary New Science of Exercise and the Brain,* went as far as to say that exercise can be just as effective as medication for some people. There are several reasons for this: First, when you engage in exercise, you turn on the region of the brain affected by ADHD and increase the flow of dopamine and other chemicals that are normally lacking. Physical activity also requires you to use the skills that you may normally struggle with, such as paying attention, maintaining focus, sequencing, following through, and using memory effectively to further activate your brain. Second, exercise produces endorphins. These are hormone-like compounds that regulate mood, causing you to feel good after an intense workout. Third relates to the idea of what psychologist Dr. Martin Seligman of the University of Pennsylvania called *learned helplessness*. Learned helplessness occurs when, after experiencing several negative consequences, a person begins to believe that he or she has no control over his or her behavior. We have touched on this idea in other chapters; these are the statements you probably replay over and over to yourself that can sabotage your efforts to change, such as "No matter what I do I'll always fail," "I am just not smart," or "I was just lucky on that one." Several studies have found exercise to prevent this phenomenon from occurring.

A modified diet can be another way to inexpensively and safely reduce your ADHD symptoms. The FDA's official stance is that there is not enough evidence to say that food additives can cause ADHD; however, some research has suggested that additives may be linked to exacerbated symptoms in people who already have ADHD. Identifying exactly which food dyes or additives might contribute to ADHD has proved more difficult. As a result, there are many proposed nutritional plans for adults with ADHD out there, and the verdict is out on exactly what approach is best. Still, a generally healthy, well-rounded diet that minimizes complex carbohydrates and maximizes high-protein and omega-3 rich foods, as well as nutrient-rich fruits and vegetables, is sure to help your brain function more effectively than one full of fatty or sugary cuisine. Whatever avenue you choose as far as your nutrition, seek the advice of a nutritionist or other medical professional who specializes in ADHD to avoid becoming victim to the latest unsubstantiated health craze.

ADHD COACHING

As discussed in Part I of this book, top ADHD expert Russell Barkley suggested that the problem for individuals with ADHD is not a skill deficit, but rather a difficulty with behavioral execution and self-regulation. He suggested that adults with the disorder may possess knowledge of coping strategies effective for most people and may have even tried some of them for themselves. However, when significant difficulty arises because of underlying executive processing mechanisms, successful performance is unachievable. These individuals find it very difficult to sacrifice an immediate reward either to gain some longer term reward or to avoid some later harm. Therefore, Barkley recommended interventions that provide a more effective course of action than teaching the use of coping mechanisms or other nonperformance-based techniques. Perhaps one of the most innovative and promising more recent intervention methods as far as life management success is ADHD coaching, which offers a more highly structured, behavioral approach than traditional counseling.

Cogmed Working Memory Training is a computerized training program designed to improve attention and concentration by increasing working memory capacity. While still relatively new, some research suggests its utility.

ADHD coaching can help you develop coping skills and strategies to resolve many of your unwanted ADHD-related behaviors, and a growing amount of research has suggested its usefulness. ADHD coaching involves helping you deal with aspects of the disorder that interfere with academic or work performance and cope with ADHD-related difficulties such as procrastination, lack of concentration, ineffective self-regulation, poor planning, anxiety, social incompetence, or time management. Useful strategies you may learn in coaching include organizational skills, time management, and specific study skills. Coaching involves setting concrete, realistic goals and can extend to many facets of your life.

Coaching is similar to traditional counseling in several ways. Both coaching and traditional counseling establish helping relationships that are supportive, respectful, and confidential; work on setting goals and assessing priorities; and require a client who is willing to make changes in his or her behavior. However, most therapists also help to guide clients toward insight, or a deeper understanding of behavior, whereas coaches may or may not do this, depending on who is doing the coaching. Coaches do not have to be licensed or formally trained, or possess a formal degree. Unlike counselors, coaches who are not also licensed mental health professionals cannot explore serious emotional, cognitive, or behavioral problems of clinical intensity, such as depression, anxiety, or substance abuse, which can often coexist with ADHD. If any emotional issues arise during the coaching process, coaches who are not licensed therapists must have resources for referring the client to a mental health professional.

Unlike counseling, coaching is far more pragmatic than many types of psychotherapy (with the exception of CBT). It is behavior oriented as opposed to insight oriented. Coaching can also be more flexible than therapy because many coaches do not require in-person meetings. The ADHD coach and client have a structured, goal-driven, strategy-oriented relationship. Goal completion and strategy building are the most important aspects of the coaching process. The focus is on developing strategies and skills to become more effective in everyday life. Each client receives individualized help. Different clients may require help in different areas of life (e.g., school, work, nutrition, exercise, stress management, and relationships). For each of these areas, the client and coach both agree on set strategies. It is the coach's job to help the client understand how ADHD impacts his or her behavior and then to encourage the client's motivation and active involvement in making changes to this behavior. The coach also elicits creative strategies to serve the needs of the client. Coach and client are in contact many times during a week to monitor progress and encourage accountability. Contact can include in-person meetings, phone calls, e-mails, or text messages. Visit http://www.nami.org/askthedoctor to listen to a 15-minute podcast about ADHD coaching featuring Dr. Levrini.

ACCOMMODATIONS

Under the Americans With Disabilities Act (ADA), anyone who has a legitimate disability has the right to seek appropriate accommodations for a wide range of physical and psychiatric disabilities, including ADHD. Accommodations may be defined as assistive devices or adaptations that serve to ease the impact of the disability on a particular activity. Several tools and devices can help you with communicating, writing, staying organized, remembering important information and dates, or keeping track of time. Accommodations may also require slight adjustments to your school or work environment in order for you to work efficiently and effectively, such as a flexible work schedule, presenting information orally rather than creating a written report, or the use of a quiet private office.

The decision to become public with your disorder and exercise your right to accommodations is a very personal one. You may, rightly so, fear discrimination and the reactions of others. Unfortunately, we live in a world where not everyone understands mental health issues. Coworkers or friends may ignorantly think ADHD is "an excuse for laziness," or a boss may not want to deal with a person who needs support. Although under the law, such a boss would be in violation, life and relationships can be tricky.

When deciding whether to request accommodations at school or work, consider the following: If a person who is physically bound to a wheelchair requests the use of a wheelchair ramp to get into his or her place of work, do you think to yourself, "They have arms! Can't they just crawl up?!" Of course not. More than likely, you think of the ramp as a way to level the playing field, so to speak—a way for the person to get from A to B with the same relative ease that you can. Similarly, you have the right to request modifications to your work environment to allow you to get from A to B with the same relative ease as your coworkers. Whether we're talking wheelchair ramps or a quiet private office to help you focus, all individuals with disabilities have the right to accommodations. Fortunately for many people, the decision to disclose their ADHD and assert their right to accommodations is the right one, and most supervisors and staff are extremely understanding and helpful.

MULTIMODAL TREATMENT

Multimodal is simply a synonym for the word *multiple*, meaning multiple methods of treatment. Experts recommend multimodal treatment for adults with ADHD, including a combination of behavioral and medical interventions to help you succeed at home, work, and school. Standard psychotherapy in conjunction with medication continues to be a popular method of dealing with symptoms. However, behavioral options can include things like coaching or neurofeedback, and these may be better options for some. The important thing to keep in mind is that medication can provide increased focus or control, and behavioral treatments can provide increased coping skills—things that medication cannot teach.

WHAT TYPE OF TREATMENT IS FOR ME?

Answer the following questions. Circle the letter or letters that best represent you for each one. When deciding on treatment, remember that multimodal (medication plus behavioral intervention) proves best.

1. How much would you pay for treatment of your ADHD symptoms?
   A. I'd rather put little or no money toward treatment.
   B. I am willing to put out several hundred dollars for treatment that has proven effective.
   C. I would pay several thousand dollars to try an up-and-coming, nontraditional approach.
   D. If it's not free, I'm not trying it.
2. What type of interaction do you prefer?
   A. I like group settings where I can bounce ideas off of many people who have experienced similar situations.

   B. I like individualized, one-on-one attention with an expert.

   C. I prefer to work with technology rather than people.

   D. I like to try things on my own that don't require professional help.

3. How much time are you willing to devote to treatment?

   A. I would like to find something ongoing but not necessarily weekly.

   B. I prefer regular weekly sessions, but ones that don't go on for years and years.

   C. I want to know exactly how many sessions my treatment will take.

   D. I don't want to spend any time outside of my home devoted to treatment.

4. How do you prefer to engage in problem solving?

   A. I like to get feedback from as many people as possible and weigh all the options.

   B. I want someone who has a lot of experience and expertise to offer their ideas.

   C. I don't like the act of trying to problem solve—I'd rather try something up and coming that requires little problem solving on my part.

   D. If it's free, I'll try it.

5. What issues do you struggle with most in terms of your ADHD?

   A. Feeling misunderstood or underappreciated

   B. Time management, organization, goal setting

   C. Focus, control, impulsivity

   D. What don't I struggle with?

Now total the number of questions for which you selected answer A. Do the same for B, C and D. If you answered mostly As, you may want to try group counseling or a support group. If you answered mostly Bs, you may want to try ADHD coaching or CBT. If you answered mostly Cs, you may want to try neurofeedback. If you answered mostly Ds, you may want to try mindfulness meditation, a nutrition and exercise regime, and the exercises in this book!

FINDING HELP

When it comes to finding a coach, therapist, or other ADHD specialist, one of the best places to start is with your friends and family, coworkers, and neighbors. Many people know someone with ADHD—be it their spouse or their best friend's dog's veterinarian's brother. Ask around to find out who they went to for treatment and what they thought of the person they saw. If no one you know can refer you to someone they have personally dealt with in the field of ADHD, you still have options.

Recommended Websites

http://www.chadd.org—CHADD (Children and Adults With ADHD) is the nation's leading nonprofit organization serving individuals with ADHD and their families. It has local chapters across the nation and a database in which you can search for all kinds of specialists in the world of ADHD, from psychiatrists to therapists to coaches. Many chapters of CHADD also offer free seminars and support groups.

http://www.psychologytoday.com—This website allows you to search for a therapist using a refined search that includes "issues" (ADHD) and "treatment orientation" (cognitive–behavioral/CBT). There is also an option to search for group therapy.

http://www.psychedcoaches.com—Psych Ed Coaches (PEC) is a nontraditional practice that combines the most effective aspects of CBT and ADHD coaching to help clients utilize their strengths and reach their goals. The website provides a description of how such a coaching approach can be helpful and who the treatment may ben efit. When looking for a coach or therapist in your area, you may benefit from using the PEC website.

Other Helpful Sources

The local university. Because ADHD affects many of today's college students, more and more university counseling centers run treatment programs or know of specialists in the area to refer to. For example, Florida State University's Adult Learning and Evaluation Center uses graduate level counseling students as ADHD coaches (http://www.epls.fsu.edu/alec/). Another benefit of going to a university is that the cost is usually far more affordable.

Medical doctors. Whether it be your family doctor, an OB/GYN, or your dentist, these medical professionals talk to dozens of people every day. They are also immersed in a world in which they often cross paths with professionals in similar fields (i.e., mental health).

School psychologists, counselors, and teachers. Similar to medical doctors, teachers and counselors gain knowledge of ADHD specialists in two ways: through experience with students and parents and through professional associations. Even if your child's teacher does not know of anyone, other staff at the school may. Most schools are required to have a school psychologist on staff to conduct testing and this person should be able to recommend where to go for treatment.

What to Ask

Once you have finally located someone you think may be a good fit for treatment of your ADHD symptoms, you are not quite done. Think of the first session or telephone consultation as an interview. He or she needs to win you over to get the job of being your professional of choice. Would you buy a car without first finding out how long it has been running, knowing the mileage, or whether it has been in any accidents? Of course not—you would be putting your life at stake. The same should go for your mental health treatment. Although your physical self may not be vulnerable during therapy or other treatment for ADHD, your psychological self is. Therefore, it is up to you to make sure that you are in the hands of an experienced, caring professional and that the method of treatment is right for you. The following is a list of just some of the possible questions you may want to ask before signing up for services:

Pretreatment Questions

1. How long have you been doing this?
2. How many clients do you see a week?
3. Are there any risks to this treatment?
4. When should I expect to see some results?
5. Why do you believe in this treatment method?
6. Are you licensed? In what? Any other credentials?
7. Can you give me the name of a former client who may be willing to speak to me?
8. What level of education do you have?
9. How much does this cost?
10. Do you accept my insurance?

What else would you like to know? Write your own questions here:

_____

_____

_____

_____

_____

_____

 HELP YOURSELF!

An important final step when deciding whether to pursue treatment for your ADHD is to ask yourself, "Is there anything holding me back from this?" Many people are too nervous or scared to seek help, whether it be because of a personal insecurity or fear of the stigma that, unfortunately, still exists in regard to seeking help with mental health. Check "yes" or "no" for each of the following statements to gauge where your fear level lies. For those you answer with "yes," read the corresponding counterthought to help you to alleviate your fear.

Fear and Insecurities Checklist

	Yes	No
1. I'm afraid people will look down on me or think I am "crazy" if I seek treatment.	☐	☐

Most people who undergo treatment for a mental health disorder are not seriously ill but rather simply need help working through some of the challenges life can present. In reality, those who are brave and self-assured enough to ask for help are far more well-adjusted than those who let their fear and insecurities keep them from reaching out.

	Yes	No
2. I'm afraid of letting go and telling someone all my deep dark secrets— I don't want them to think I am a bad person.	☐	☐

True professionals do not judge their clients. In fact, a professional will most likely respect and appreciate your ability to be honest. Furthermore, no matter how terrible you think your secret is, chances are your treatment provider has heard much worse!

	Yes	No
3. I'm afraid that treatment will change me. I like some of my ADHD personality traits—they make me who I am.	☐	☐

Specialists who work with clients with ADHD do so because they enjoy and appreciate the personality traits that often accompany the client, such as charisma, energy, enthusiasm, creativity, and easygoingness. Treatment for

---

ADHD aims only to affect change on the symptoms that negatively impact your life, not those that you appreciate or consider a part of your personality.

4. I'm afraid that seeking treatment means I am weak—shouldn't I be able to handle my own problems? □ □

It takes an incredibly strong person to ask for and accept help from others. Plus, sometimes it takes a fresh outside perspective to help you see things you cannot. Furthermore, most professionals who specialize in ADHD and mental health go to school for a very long time and work with people similar to you day in and day out, so they have gained a bit of extra knowledge and are eager to share.

5. I'm afraid of what I might uncover during treatment—what if I'm worse than I thought? □ □

Chances are you won't and you aren't. However, anything you might uncover in treatment that you previously did not know about yourself can only help. Even if you did not know it on a conscious level, it was there somewhere, festering and affecting your life. Once issues are brought to the surface, they can be dealt with in a healthy, effective way.

6. Other: _____

_____

_____

Counterthought: _____

_____

_____

_____

7. Other: _____

_____

_____

Counterthought: _____

_____

_____

_____

SUMMARY

Here are the important points you will want to take away from this chapter. Use the following checklist to note the areas you have thoroughly studied. Leave the box empty if it is an area you would like to come back to and review further.

☐ I understand what my (nonpharmacological) treatment options are.

☐ I have considered which type of treatment is for me.

☐ I have learned ways to locate a specialist in my area.

☐ I have learned how to "interview" a potential specialist before committing to treatment.

☐ I have learned how to overcome any lingering fears that I have in regard to asking for or receiving professional help.

SUMMARY

Congratulations! You've read all or parts of this book and are clearly committed to achieving your goals and better managing your life. Living with ADHD is a challenge, but one that has many positive aspects. Throughout our professional practice, we have found that we really like working with adults who have ADHD. You tend to be interesting, creative, exciting, upbeat, and full of surprises. Sure, there are things that need some work, but we have found that with the right support, education, and encouragement, adults with ADHD can make drastically positive improvements in their lives. We hope that after reading this book, you agree. We hope that you have selected those areas that are most important to you and have tried many of the strategies. You should be used to taking our quizzes by now, so here's a final one; we hope that most of your answers will be "yes"!

1. Have you set at least one specific goal for your life?
2. Have you tried setting some weekly objectives in order to reach a goal?
3. Have you learned some specific things that motivate you and also discarded some things that don't work as motivators for you?
4. If you are still in school, have you tried a new strategy for studying, taking tests, or writing a paper?
5. If you are employed, have you tried a new strategy that has helped you with timeliness, focusing, or getting your work done?
6. Can you think of a new behavior or insight about yourself that has helped you with your relationships with others?
7. Can you describe one way in which you are better organized?
8. Can you name one thing you have learned about managing your time?
9. If you think you might have difficulties with stress, anxiety, or depression, have you attempted one self-help strategy to lessen your symptoms? If that didn't work, can you identify an outside source of help that you think you might follow up on?
10. If you take medication for ADHD, do you think you're at that optimal point at which you're on the right medication and the right dose, and your side effects are minimal?

We're betting that you were able to answer "yes" to at least half of the 10 questions. We would characterize that as a great success! But one thing we've learned working with our clients with ADHD is that progress is measured in small steps and managing your life takes perseverance. So here are some final tips. First, for every question you answered "yes," celebrate your success, give yourself a big pat on the back, and relish the thought that you are capable of succeeding with adult ADHD. But be aware that new behaviors need practice, and don't be discouraged if you backslide a bit. Get in the habit of reviewing the things that are working for you, keeping at them, and practicing them, and watch them gradually become the usual and standard way of living your life. After a while they will become habits, part of who you are, rather than behaviors you have to work at.

Second, for each of the questions you answered "no," ask yourself if it matters. Maybe that's not an area that you need help with. We would not be surprised if not every chapter in this book is something you want to work on. Did you find one that still needs work? Well, let that be your next goal. Tackle that area just like you did the areas that you've successfully changed. Read the chapter again if necessary. Admit it, did you skip the exercises or not really try too hard? Give it another try. We find it very common that our clients are successful after one or more attempts at a goal. Are you convinced that you just can't quite manage it on your own? Perhaps it's time to follow the advice in Chapter 10 and seek some outside help or consult some of the references in the Further Reading section. There are many good resources out there and many professionals with expertise in ADHD who can give you that extra help you need.

Finally, we want to thank those of you with ADHD who have filled our professional lives. We couldn't have written this book without you. Your stories, your hard work, and your courage inspire us. We are gratified to be a part of your life, and hope that this book helps you to manage your life in the best way possible.

FURTHER READING

ADHD OVERVIEW

American Psychological Association. *Psychology topics: ADHD*. Retrieved from http://www.apa.org/topics/adhd/index.aspx

Children and Adults With Attention Deficit/Hyperactivity Disorder. *Adults with AD/HD: Steps for beginners*. Retrieved from http://www.chadd.org/AM/Template.cfm?Section=Especially_For_Adults

Baruchin, A. (2008, March 12). Attention deficits that may linger well past childhood. *The New York Times*. Retrieved from http://www.nytimes.com

Rabiner, D. *Diagnostic criteria for ADD/ADHD*. Retrieved from http://www.helpforadd.com/criteria-for-add/

GOAL SETTING

Barkley, R. (1997). *ADHD and the nature of self-control*. New York, NY: Guilford Press.

Mehlman, B. (2008, August 19). Goal setting for ADHD adults [Blog post]. *ADDitude Treating ADHD Blog.* Retrieved from http://www.additude mag.com/adhdblogs/3/4166.html

Locke's Goal Setting Theory. *MindTools.* Retrieved from http://www.mind tools.com/pages/article/newHTE_87.htm

SPECIFIC SKILLS

Austin, W. J. (2001). *10 keys to time management.* Retrieved from http://www.coachville.com/tl/thomasleonard/karla/formsCD/161keysto timemanagement.pdf

Children and Adults With Attention Deficit/Hyperactivity Disorder. *Adults with ADHD and relationships.* Retrieved from http://www.chadd. org/Content/CHADD/EFAdults/ADDultRelationships/default.htm

Covey, S. (1989). *The seven habits of highly successful people: Powerful lessons in personal change.* New York, NY: Simon & Schuster.

Dartmouth University, Academic Skills Center. *Improving concentration, memory, and motivation.* Retrieved from http://www.dartmouth.edu/ ~acskills/success/study.html

Dawson, P., & Guare, R. (2000). *Coaching the ADHD student.* North Tonawanda, NY: Multi-Health Systems.

Fellman, W. (2000). *Finding a career that works for you.* Plantation, FL: Specialty Press.

Fellman, W. R. *Making ADHD-friendly career choices.* Retrieved from http://w3.addresources.org/?q=node/271

Hallowell, E., Hallowell, S., & Orlov, M. (2010). *Married to distraction: Restoring intimacy and strengthening your marriage in an age of interruption.* New York, NY: Ballantine Books.

Kansas State University, Counseling Services. *Study strategies.* Retrieved from http://www.k-state.edu/counseling/topics/career/studystr.htm

Kolberg, J., & Nadeau, K. (2002). *ADD-friendly ways to organize your life.* New York, NY: Brunner-Routledge.

Low, K. (2009, April 6). *Time management tips for adults with ADHD.* Retrieved from http://add.about.com/od/adhdinadults/a/running late.htm

Low, K. (2010, March 8). *Work tips from adults with ADHD.* Retrieved from http://add.about.com/od/adhdinadults/a/Work-and-ADD_2.htm

Nadeau, K. G. (1996). *ADD in the workplace.* Bristol, PA: Brunner/Mazel.
National Resource Center on ADHD. *Succeeding in the workplace.* Retrieved
from http://www.help4adhd.org/en/living/workplace/WWK16
Pauk, W. (2000). *Essential study strategies.* Clearwater, FL: H&H.
Purdue University Online Writing Lab. http://owl.english.purdue.edu
Rapaport, W. J. (2011, September 28). *How to study: A brief guide.* Retrieved
from http://www.cse.buffalo.edu/~rapaport/howtostudy.html
Robinson, F. P. (1970). *Effective study* (4th ed.). New York, NY: Harper &
Row. (The SQ3R Reading Method)
Susan, P. (2006). *Organizing solutions for people with attention deficit
disorder.* Gloucester, MA: Quayside Publishing Group.
Virginia Tech, Cook Counseling Center. http://www.ucc.vt.edu/

TREATMENT

Brynes, G., & Watkins, W. (2007). *Attention deficit in adults: It rarely travels
alone.* Retrieved from http://www.ncpamd.com/ADDComorbidity.htm
National Resource Center on ADHD. *ADHD and coexisting disorders
(WWK 5).* Retrieved from http://www.help4adhd.org/en/treatment/
coexisting/WWK5
Ramsay, J. R. (2010). *Nonmedication treatments for adult ADHD: Evalu-
ating impact on daily functioning and well-being.* Washington, DC:
American Psychological Association.
Ramsey, R., & Rostain, A. (2008). *Cognitive-behavioral therapy for adult
ADHD: An integrative psychosocial and medical approach.* New York,
NY: Routledge.
Ratey, J. (2008). Spark: *The revolutionary new science of exercise and the
brain.* New York, NY: Little Brown and Company.
WebMD. *Overview of ADHD in adults.* Retrieved from http://www.webmd.
com/add-adhd/guide/adhd-adults

INDEX

ABOUT THE AUTHORS

Abigail Levrini, PhD, is a clinical psychologist and owner of Psych Ed Coaches, a northern Virginia/DC-based private practice specializing in ADHD coaching and cognitive–behavioral treatment. Dr. Levrini has presented her research and coaching model at professional settings throughout the country and frequently lectures and conducts workshops at scientific conferences, schools, and public forums throughout the United States. Dr. Levrini is also the current Board Leader for the DC/Northern VA Chapter of CHADD (Children and Adults With ADHD). Further information about Dr. Levrini and Psych Ed Coaches is available at http://www.psychedcoaches.com.

Frances Prevatt, PhD, is a professor in the Department of Educational Psychology and Learning Systems at Florida State University and the Executive Director of the Adult Learning Evaluation Center (ALEC). ALEC provides assessments and interventions to college students and young adults with ADHD, provides training to graduate students, and is the setting for many research projects dealing with ADHD. She was on the faculty at Texas A&M University for 15 years before moving to Florida State University. Dr. Prevatt has authored over 70 publications in the field of educational psychology. Further information about Dr. Prevatt and ALEC can be found at http://www.epls.fsu.edu/alec/.